9 Lies

That Are
Holding
Your Business
Back...

...and the TRUTH That Will Set It Free

9 Lies

That Are
Holding
Your Business
Back ...

...and the TRUTH That Will Set It Free

By STEVE CHANDLER
&
SAM BECKFORD

CAREER
PRESS

Franklin Lakes, NJ

9 Lies That Are Holding Your Business Back
Edited and Typeset by Christopher Carolei
Cover design by Lu Rossman / Digi Dog Design
Printed in the U.S.A. by Book-mart Press

To order this title, please call toll-free 1-800-CAREER-1 (NJ and Canada: 201-848-0310) to order using VISA or MasterCard, or for further information on books from Career Press.

The Career Press, Inc., 3 Tice Road, PO Box 687,
Franklin Lakes, NJ 07417
www.careerpress.com

Library of Congress Cataloging-in-Publication Data

Chandler, Steve. 1944-

9 lies that are holding your business back : ...and the truth that will set it free / Steve Chandler and Sam Beckford.

    p. cm.

Includes bibliographical references and index.

ISBN 1-56414-836-X (cloth)

1. Success in business. 2. New business enterprises. 3. Self-actualization (Psychology) 4. Motivation (Psychology) I. Title: Nine lies that are holding your business back. II. Beckford, Sam. III. Title.

HF5386.C476 2005

658.4'09--dc22

2005051324

Dedication

To Valerie
—Sam

To Kathy
—Steve

Acknowledgments

To my father who taught me that the crowds stop at the bottom of the mountain, but there is always room at the top. To my mother who taught me that being free in spirit is the only way to be alive. To Dave for your friendship and support. To Jose for being a friend, father figure, and cheering section. To Dan Kennedy for showing me the elevator and helping me skip the stairs. To Ross and Marty Simons for sharing your story and being an encouragement to small business owners everywhere. To Steve for finally showing me what I want to be when I grow up. To Kathy Chandler for your contribution and ideas. And above all, to my wife, Valerie, the best partner I could hope for in business and in life.

—Sam Beckford

To my coauthor Sam Beckford, "The Small Business Millionaire," and the man who has helped so many small businesses find their way. To Steve Hardison, the best life coach on the planet and my best man. To Hameed Ali for the diamonds, to Darby Checketts for delivering Archimedes, to Ron Fry for so many years of publishing excellence, to Michael Lewis for the faith, to Ron and Mary Hulnick and all the soul-centered leaders at The University of Santa Monica, and to Kathryn Anne Eimers Chandler, for whom there are no words.

—Steve Chandler

The common idea that success spoils people by making them vain, egotistic, and self-complacent is erroneous; on the contrary, it makes them, for the most part, humble, tolerant and kind. Failure makes people bitter and cruel.

—W. Somerset Maugham

Contents

Introduction

The Loan Officer
Who Didn't Believe

Flashback: May 1996

"I'm sorry, but we can't lend your business $7,000," the 30-something loan officer said as he shook his head sadly. He continued on: "80 percent of businesses fail in the first five years, and your business is too risky for our bank to take a chance on. How do you know your business will even make it?"

My wife Valerie and I were disappointed and felt insulted, but how could we respond?

Because the loan officer had a point. We had no collateral. Our only asset was a "beater" Honda hatchback with almost 200,000 miles on it, and that wasn't even paid for. We also still had debts from my previous five failed business attempts and my actual income on my 1994 tax return was zero. Hardly an encouraging fact sheet to present to him.

Although our current business was doing almost $4,000 per month in sales, that was not overly impressive to him, and we were only taking out about $1,900 per month for ourselves. We didn't really look like a winning horse to bet on.

But still, his words hurt.

As we drove home to our apartment, our disappointment was soon replaced by anger and determination. Why get down about this? We both decided right then and there that our business *was* going to make it and we *were* going to be successful. We'd show him!

Update: May 2005

Our business has grown to a stable $250,000 per month. Our net worth is approaching the two million dollar mark. We are living in a $500,000 house and driving two $50,000 cars. The beater Honda and that conversation with the loan officer seem very far away in time. But emotionally, that moment is still very close.

How did all this happen? What exactly did we do?

Read on, because that's what this book is about. If you want to be in the 20 percent of small business owners who live the dream and experience success, this book will tell you how. If we can do it, so can you. How do I know this? Because I've taught hundreds of others how to do *exactly* what we did. There's nothing special about us, but there *is* something special about what happens when you learn these truths.

We will not only tell you how we did it but we will combine our ideas with strategies from the nation's leading expert on the psychology of personal success, Steve Chandler. His innovative book *100 Ways to Motivate Yourself* has been a bestseller throughout the world for 10 years in a row and is now available in 11 languages.

But there's no point in just reading about someone else's success if you can't convert it into action for your own business. This book will show you how to do that, and how to follow through. And then it will show you how to keep on succeeding into the future.

—Sam Beckford

PS. If you're the loan officer from that 1996 meeting, and you get this book, thanks, but we don't need to borrow the $7,000 anymore.

Lie

I Just Need to Know *How* to Do This

We are about to tell you precisely you how to succeed in business. But there is something that must be handled before that. Something so important that to skip it would be a crime.

Most people do skip it. Most people jump right in, trying to figure out *how to* succeed in their business, as if that was all they really needed to know. But it's not true. There's something else that they need, even more important than the *how to*…and that's the *want to*.

Don't proceed in your business without a *want* to succeed. Don't even go to work if you don't have it. You're better off closing the place down for a day and taking a long, long walk to ask yourself, "Why do I want this to succeed?"

Then answer that question by listing lots of benefits that will accrue to you and your family by your succeeding at this business—not just getting by, but succeeding. Talk to yourself about this. Have this conversation with yourself and later write down the answers where you can look at them each day.

This is a conversation a lovely young woman by the name of Francine never had with herself. Of course, we don't know that for sure, but the signs were all there that she never got clear about the depth of her intention.

Francine opened a franchise coffee shop five minutes away from one of the locations of Sam's business. He was in her shop getting coffee one day after she opened and he struck up a conversation with her.

"I run the business down the street," said Sam. "How are things going here?"

"Things are going well," said Francine, and for someone who was starting a new business, she looked pretty successful already. She was well-dressed, not in the regular franchise uniform, and the $40,000 car in the parking lot was hers. Sam had seen her getting out of it before.

On a later visit, Sam learned that she co-owned the business with her father, who had put up all the investment to get things going. (So the car and the clothes started making more sense.) Sam himself had just finished a record year in his small business down the street and was in the process of expanding. In the following months, he stopped in the coffee shop often but Francine wasn't around as much, and when she was there she was always in the back doing computer work. She was no longer out front talking with customers. Sam caught her eye one day as she peeked out from the back room and he asked again how business was.

"Things are slow," said Francine. "But I think it's the economy. The economy is slow, so what can you do?"

Sam didn't know how to answer her because he'd just finished a record year! He was in the same neighborhood, working inside the same economy. But was it slow? The area they were in had new construction happening all around! And there were local area statistics just out that revealed the large number of new residents moving into the area. Sam was in the middle of preparing his increased advertising to match the influx. What economy was Francine talking about?

A few months later Sam noticed that Francine's shop had reduced the serving staff to cut back on payroll expenses. When he went in for coffee, it took a little longer to get served. Sam saw her getting out of her expensive car one day as he was leaving the shop.

"Things going well?" Sam asked.

"No, it's worse than ever," said Francine. "There just isn't a customer base to draw from. I've tried. In an economy like this, you don't have a lot to work with. People don't have a lot of extra money to go out and spend."

Not long after that, Sam parked his car down the street, came by the store and noticed that the door was padlocked. Francine's store was no longer in business.

And here's an ironic footnote: The store location wasn't shut down for long before there was another coffee shop franchise operating successfully out of her same location.

Soon two other good coffee shops opened, each one about five minutes away!

It was clear that Francine never got grounded in her intention to succeed. Searching wildly for her *how to*, she had never strengthened her *want to*. Her intention had only gone this far: "I'll open this place and see what happens." That's an intention, of sorts, but it is not enough. You have to *want to* succeed. If you *want to* badly enough, you'll always find the *how to*. And once you've got your *want to* tuned up and ready to operate, outside forces (such as the "economy") won't be an issue.

Whenever a small business owner has a weak *want to* on the inside, all power goes to the outside. That's why the missing *want to* is never identified as the problem. Having a weak *want to* inside will create an exaggerated fear of the forces outside of you: competition, the economy, location, employee problems, lack of cash investment, all those outside forces that appear strong only when the inside is weak.

We humans often make this common mistake: We jump to the *how to* way too soon! We buy books on how to lose weight, without really wanting to lose weight. When we do this we are ignoring something even more important than the *how to*, and that's having a strong enough *want to*.

Most people, once they get their business up and running—whether it's cleaning gutters, washing windows, or selling rebuilt cars, it doesn't matter—just come to work and stay busy inside that business all day and then go home. If they notice that things aren't getting any traction, they start to look around outside of themselves for answers. Maybe they bounce around from one advertising representative to the next, or from one relative to the next, asking, "How do I make this thing work?"

But they don't realize that a "system" is not what's missing. *How to* make it work is not what's missing. What's primarily missing is a strong intention to succeed. And what that lack of intention gets filled with inside a human being is an intention to just "keep my job" and get through the day.

People can turn this whole purpose deficit around if they just check their intentions as they go to work: *What's my intention today?* To just keep this job? To just keep this small business I've created for myself and my family and get through the day without too much damage done? *Or is my intention to succeed?* And if my intention is to succeed, grow the business, and indeed maybe even become a millionaire, then I will think completely differently every step of the way.

If your small business career is not yet what you want it to be, it may be that "Intention Deficit Disorder" (no real clarity about what result you intend to produce), is the biggest problem you have, and the first problem that needs to be solved.

Let's look at this another way. If your teenage son's room is chronically messy it would probably never occur to you to send him to a seminar on "how to clean a room." The reason you wouldn't is based on your knowledge that the "how to" is not missing here. The "want to" is missing. You know that. He doesn't want to clean his room. The only way you will get him to clean his room is to create an incentive—through pain or gain—that makes him want to clean his room. And you need to do the same for yourself. Your business requires a strong intention to succeed.

Don't Just Figure Out *How to* Do It

We have sometimes given small business owners a multitude of fresh ideas on how to add value to their services and raise prices accordingly. We know that by using these ideas, they will turn their cash flow around and begin to prosper. We know this. But when we check back with them later, we often find they've tried almost none of the ideas. We then realize that we went to the *how to* too soon.

A young man named Reggie recently approached us during a seminar and said that our ideas sounded fine but that the economy in his town was so bad that his business was not going to make it. After working with him for a while, we thought we had succeeded in giving Reggie a number of ways to actually leverage the slow economy to his advantage with his customers and have his business come out smelling like a rose.

But we still couldn't get the sadness out of his voice or the victim look out of his eyes. It was almost as if Reggie had already chosen his fate and chosen his emotional response to having his own business.

We all of a sudden realized that Reggie didn't *want to* succeed. Not yet, anyway. So we would have to address that deficit first.

We believe that one of the reasons our Website programs and teleseminars are now working at such a dramatic level is we address the *how to* and the *want to* with equal attention and commitment. Sam Beckford's well-chronicled success as a small business millionaire, and his follow-up success at teaching all his secrets on *how to* do exactly what he did, are synergistically woven together with my personal motivation coaching (the *want to*) so that both halves of a successful small business owner can emerge.

A person must have both the *how to* and the *want to* to succeed. Both traits can be taught, and both can be learned.

The *want to* is often the most important component of your success, especially if it's missing! To succeed at anything, you have to want it. But most people overlook this simple fact. And when they are confronted about the fact that their actions suggest that they don't really want to succeed, they get very depressed. They believe there is something wrong with them. But there is nothing wrong with them. All they need is for their level of desire to get a tune-up. Anyone can do it. We keep proving that.

Your level of *want to* is totally within your control. It doesn't exist by itself. You are in charge of its intensity. You can turn the flame up or down any time you want.

But most people don't realize that one's desire to succeed isn't a permanent thing. Similarly, they think it's some character flaw or personality trait in them when they aren't driven to succeed. But it's not. Desire and intention are living, growing, ever-changing energy sources inside you. You can learn to continuously grow them to any degree you want. You can learn to motivate yourself to whatever degree of energy and enthusiasm you choose. Outside events have nothing to do with it. Personal history has nothing to do with it. It lives at the level of choice. You have the power to choose it.

How to Get What You Really Want

If there is a level of business success that you want but do not have, then the first place to look for it is in your deepest self. Why do you want this business to succeed? What good things would it do? Do you think you deserve it yet? If not, why in the world don't you? (And if your answers are opening up more and more clarity for your objective, then you are getting somewhere. If they are not, then you need to step back in space and time and start out in a more primal way. How do other people motivate themselves? How can I learn to do that? See our Website to get more information about these questions.)

Some people leave their job in a big company because they think they have enough *want to* to start a small business. They leave the security of a regular paycheck for the adventure of the entrepreneurial world. But after the first few difficulties their *want to* begins to weaken and outside forces seem to acquire more and more power over them.

Brandon was just such an individual. He was a successful sales manager in pharmaceuticals in Michigan when he decided to strike out on his own. He had an excellent business plan for a small technical supply shop, so he moved his wife and family to Florida to start afresh.

Difficulties hit him early. Brandon's business partner turned out to be unimaginative and not very motivated. The early money invested in the project began to run out faster than anticipated. Sales were slow, and Brandon began to long for his former sense of confidence. Things at home weren't all that great now either, especially now that he was bringing his fears home. And soon it was just a matter of time before the whole thing came down around him like a house of cards.

Today Brandon (after closing down his failed business) has found a secure middle-management position with a large company in Florida, and his life is getting back to normal. When we talk to him now, we can hear that he still doesn't fully understand what happened to his small business. He still talks about what he thinks happened outside of him, but he is still clueless about what happened inside.

"If I ever do that kind of thing again," says Brandon, "I'll start with more money up front. I never gave myself a chance to get rolling. We only had a year, and everyone knows it takes four years before you see a profit in a business."

Brandon is quick to identify the many outside forces that got in his way.

"My partner and employees weren't what I had hoped," he says today. "I think that was what also doomed the enterprise. I needed someone with a lot more confidence and energy to work with. And finally, we entered the market at just the wrong time. Most of our potential clients had already signed their supply contracts for the year so we just had to bide our time."

During this period of time we had given Brandon numerous ideas about how to jump-start his business, but he was too uninspired to give them a real fair try. He had already lost his *want to*, so, of course, all of our *how to* ideas fell on deaf ears.

I made a mistake as a coach. I didn't get Brandon as clear as I could have up front about his intention. I assumed too much about his level of desire to succeed and proceeded too quickly to the specifics. That's a mistake I will not make again. Without the desire, no system—no matter how brilliant—can work.

Learning to Want to Have a Great Team

Doug and Jan had been doing well enough with their franchised furniture store in Fresno, California, but one month the bottom fell out when a number of sales people ("designers") quit for various reasons, leaving them short-handed and cash poor.

We began coaching them in our principles for small business success, but realized that for the principles to work, a quick shock to the system was needed.

"Good people are hard to find," said Doug, "and we're losing sales every day now because we don't have good sales people to capitalize on the people who come into the store."

"Good people are hard to find when you need them," I said, in our first heart-to-heart coaching session. "And your problem is that you always wait until you need them to start looking for them. That's why you are struggling."

"How do you find good people?" asked Jan, reflecting her husband's frustration.

"It's not a matter of *how to*," I said. "There is no problem learning how to find good people. That's not what's missing here."

"We don't follow you," said Doug.

"Your business struggles...because you hire to fill needs," I asked. "You do what's needed. You don't do what's wanted, you do what's needed. It's a needs-based activity. It's counter-productive. You get nowhere. All that work and all that time and you keep sliding back to ground zero. That's what needs-based activity does."

"Well," said Doug. "It's true, though. We do need people. If we had a few more people like our top person Michelle, we'd be in the money right now. Because of the shortage, Jan and I have to be in here ourselves all week from early morning to night. Even on Saturdays."

I wanted to drive his point home. "Until you proactively *create* the company you want, you will always have a major struggle on your hands," I said. "Also, it is not true that the owners need to give so much of their precious time to the business. That is only true if your recruitment is reaction-based instead of a creation. Most small businesses Sam Beckford and I coach create a way for the owners to come by once a week. That's plenty!"

"That would be heaven," Jan said. She and Doug had just adopted a little boy and hated the thought that they hardly saw him during the day anymore.

"For now, during this period, I agree that you must be there full-time," I said. "Talking to customers, saving your business, and so on. It is perfectly appropriate during this current crisis. However, if the two of you *commit* to being great at recruiting and hiring you will have people who want to do what you're now doing, and who can do it well."

Doug and Jan were not persuaded. I had to confront them about how much time they had blocked out on their calendars for recruiting and hiring in the past year, and of course the answer was zero. They scurried around interviewing people whenever the need presented itself, but never proactively.

"In your business," I said, "there is no commitment right now whatsoever for building a great team. Not that there isn't a wish and a hope, there's just no commitment. There is reaction to crisis, and choosing to have your hiring be in the 'reaction' mode, rather than the 'creation' mode has caused almost every problem you have. It has tied everybody up, including yourselves."

Doug and Jan started taking notes.

"You must hear this," I said. "Simply because all the other franchise people echo your 'truth' about staffing and labor shortages doesn't make it true. Your efforts at recruiting have been disorganized and frantic, and if you had 'enough' staff you would not recruit at all. I bet there are days when you don't do any recruiting activities at all. Maybe even weeks. But it's the most important thing you could do. It's the best use of your time."

Doug and Jan began to protest about how many problems they had to deal with prior to recruiting and building a good team. As so many other business owners are, they were so "into the forest and trees" of their business they couldn't see what would give them more profit. They literally couldn't see it!

Doug and Jan had a choice. Their choice was to (1) manage an endless stream of mediocre people, trying to make this thing work, or (2) build a great team that earned them a huge profit and only required one day a week from each of them.

"That sounds impossible," said Doug.

But Jan was starting to get it.

"Doug, wait a minute, think this through," she said. "If we *had* to do it, we would. Wouldn't we? If Donald Trump brought his TV cameras into town and gave us three months to find these people, we would find them. Wouldn't we? If he said the end prize was a few million dollars?"

"Well, yeah," said Doug.

"Do you know why?" I asked. "You would be committed! It would be a completely different ball game than you have right now. Right now there's no commitment whatsoever, none, to do this. I mean it! I don't mean it as a criticism, because 90 percent of small businesses do it just like you do! And I bet that 98 percent of your franchises do it just like you do…all activities of the owners being *need-based*. Responding to what's needed to keep the business afloat. It's ironic, but *filling the needs of your businesses* is not what will ever make you successful. That's the ultimate flaw of working *in* your business rather than working *on* it. You need to focus on *wants*, not needs."

The next week Doug and Jan went on a recruiting blitz. They blocked out an hour a day to call everyone they knew in town to put the word out that they were looking, like the Marines, for "a few good (wo)men." They ran an ad in the newspaper and hung doorhangers on the doors in the nice neighborhoods of Fresno with a big picture of Michelle, their best salesperson/designer.

"Michelle had no previous experience..." said the ad, "and you don't need it either! Come take our test, and if you show you have an aptitude for design we will invite you to submit an application for a design/sales position with our company. Write to us today! Tell us about yourself. Do you watch HGTV? Do you have a love and passion for interior design and creating artful solutions for people? Why sit at home, or work in an unfulfilling job when you could work at this wonderful store! We train you thoroughly. You'll become masterful at serving our customers!"

Doug and Jan had realized that they could no longer afford to have "No one wants to work here" as the store's culture. That's what their culture had become! That's what even the best and most optimistic people they had were thinking and speaking. Their new commitment to recruiting was changing their store's entire culture.

"People listen to committed people," I had said to them. "Your employees listened to the malcontents who quit your store because those people were *committed* to being right about how hard it was to work at your store. Your people don't listen to you, because you have no waiting list of people who want to work for you. In fact, you yourselves tell them that there is a staffing crisis and a labor shortage. In your own way you are telling them 'no one wants to work here.' I'm not trying to insult you; I am trying to *wake you up* to what you are doing to your people when you don't recruit. Only you can change it around to "everyone wants to work here." Once you change it, morale, productivity, and everything else will pick up dramatically. I promise you this is true. I've worked on this very same recruitment subject with many,

many businesses, and it's *the most difficult* realization they get. It's the hardest thing to convert to: working *on* your business instead of working *in* your business. If you make the conversion, I promise you that you will double your profits. I'll help you in this project. I am committed to showing you the way to design and create the business you want and eliminate the word *crisis* from your vocabulary."

Soon Doug and Jan had three new people working in the store, and two more on their way in. Not only that, there was the beginning of a waiting list.

I stopped in the store to talk to Jan about the record sales month they had just experienced.

"Wow!" I said. "Look at how much you have done already! Great work. Stay on the phone, and network like *crazy*...until *all* of Fresno knows you are looking for a few good women. Never stop looking...never stop creating your team. Your team of people is your most important creation, it's your most important work! Way to go."

"Thanks, but may I ask you something delicate?" Jan said.

"Sure, of course," I said.

"It's always been my desire to have a very close group of trusted employees—*family,*" said Jan. "And I still have a hard time changing that mindset. So it's hard to picture a constant stream of new people always being recruited. I want to build something and keep it. I don't like change. I like the family feeling."

"Don't change that mindset," I said. "That's a great mindset! But even family members move on, and you can have a great family and a waiting list too. In fact, your waiting list will help you keep more of the family you want to keep. They will be less likely to leave, not more, if they know there are people dying to take their place. Have recruiting become your specialty, what you and Doug are known for. It will build the family you want."

Ben Didn't Have a Sporting Chance

An acquaintance of ours named Ben owns two independent sporting goods stores. He gives good customer service, and Sam has bought a few things there over the years. Sam recently asked Ben how business was going and Ben brought up the sore subject of his main competitor across town.

The competitor was also a small independent sporting goods store with two locations.

Ben said his competitors were starting to "private label" their own brand of sport shirts and track suits by dealing directly with a manufacturer. He said that they were probably making a better profit by their new approach. Ben thought they were pretty aggressive and admitted that some of their private label push was cutting into his business.

Sam then asked Ben if it would be difficult to start a private label program of his own.

"I guess it would be possible," Ben said in a weary voice. "I'd have to call a manufacturer and make some designs and test it out. I guess a guy could do it if he really wanted to."

Sam waited for the obvious, the spark of enthusiasm at this new opportunity to level the playing field. Sam hoped

Ben would say, "I'll start tomorrow. If they can do it, so can I!"

But those words never came. Ben eventually just changed the subject and started talking about the good old days of the business.

The worst failure we see business owners making is the failure that comes from no longer having the internal flame, from no longer being *willing* to try a new strategy. You can give someone all the best new strategies in the world, but if his or her willingness is not there, it won't matter. Notice this in yourself. Don't "try" something new until you've tuned yourself up for it. Take care of your own internal flame before you halfheartedly try a new system or idea.

Don't get down there with Ben and the broken spirit his low energy voice tones conveyed when he said, "I guess I could try that idea out if I wanted to, but...."

The lack of *want to* becomes a lack of oxygen! You've got to have oxygen to keep a body alive. The word *inspire* literally means "to breathe in" and businesses need daily inspiration. That's your primary responsibility. That's why we give all of our clients a deep wake-up call on the *want to* so that the *how to* has a chance to be executed. Some of the most effective teaching tools our small business owners have utilized have been dialogues Sam and I created about how to use ongoing personal self-motivation for small business success.

If you've ever lacked a fresh infusion of intention, you know what it feels like. Before your *want to* was firmly in place, you were probably similar to most business owners, going around thinking, "These customers are a *pain*, and I hope nothing *bad* happens today because I just have to put out fires. We're just battling against everything!" You were going out each morning knowing you were going to get beat up throughout your business day. Then when the day was done, you would drag yourself home and just try to forget about it.

But that is not a creative cycle. Each day the negativity and sense of overwhelm just starts all over again, and this negative will eventually destroy your business. Soon everyone associated with your little business is just working for the weekend! "Is it Wednesday yet? Good! Wednesday is hump day. We're over the hump." But wait a minute! Doesn't that sound a little familiar to you? Wasn't that why you left that big corporation you were working for? What's going on here? How could you be reproducing the same thing? You started this little business for the freedom it would give you, and it's given you the opposite!

All the Effort Is Wasted on the Start-Up

In most businesses, people set up their business and then believe that all the real important work has been done in the start-up. They think, "Once we start the business and we get it running, then we'll just come around and manage this thing."

But successful businesses don't work that way. Businesses are living things, not fixed constructions. They need to grow, just as a planted garden does. In business, it's grow or go. And by "grow" we don't necessarily mean grow larger. You can succeed by just growing better! But grow.

Your business has to be continually reinvented. You have to *want to* (want to!) continually reinvent your business so that it is better and better each day. Each day. The market is changing, the customers are changing, and every business can be improved each day to better match up, and even be ahead of, the changes.

So when you *want to* succeed, the start-up starts again every day. Every day is a new beginning. You don't ever try to nail it down. You know you can't just do the same thing. If you see a business that is doing the exact same thing today as it was five years ago, chances are that business isn't doing very well. There's nothing worse than a business that's been around for years (barely surviving) that *looks like* it's been around for years. So when the customers walk into the business they say, "Wow, this place is looking pretty rough. The carpet's in bad shape. Look at the duct tape on the carpet! That's an interesting touch. All this stuff in here is worn out. Hey, somebody tell these owners, paint is cheap! I'm sure there would be a spare weekend to paint it."

One of the reasons businesses get that weary look to them is that the owners *think of the business as something that is already done.* They think, "Okay, this is all the business is and this is all it can be." So they can't see beyond that thought. They can't even begin to ask the question, "How can this be the dream that I wanted it to be?" They miss the gold that's lying around the next corner. They miss the fact that there's so much freedom and flexibility in owning your own business that you can make it into anything you want it to be. But you have to realize that you have that power to transform the business and be willing (to generate the willingness) to make it into what you want.

This Is Your Ultimate Investment

Ralph Waldo Emerson said, "Nothing great was ever created without enthusiasm," and so to create a great success with your business you invest enthusiasm. It's your most important investment. It's the key element in the mix.

The word *enthusiasm* comes from the Greek "en theos," which means "the god within," which is the level you need to play at to win big. To succeed in business you need to bring your highest, most spiritual self to work each day. It's that vital. Your mission is to make this business your greatest piece of work ever. Your masterpiece! A monument to your energy, to your laughter and tears, to your heart and soul.

From that level you can fly. From that level, you can be so enthusiastic about serving your customer that you are continuously finding ways to astonish him or her. You can be enthusiastic about recruiting and hiring the best team of people alive. You look at all the wonderful ways you can acknowledge them and keep them in the game of pleasing your customers. You can honor their innovation and energy.

And, finally, you are enthusiastic about yourself. You have found your fun. You have become a success in life.

As journalist Sheila Graham quite wisely said, "You can have anything you want if you want it desperately enough. You must want it with an inner exuberance that erupts through the skin and joins the energy that created the world."

Enthusiasm comes from taking ownership of your life energy. You know how to do that. You did it every day as a small child. Enthusiasm comes from despising that weak, meek little voice in you that wants to be a victim of circumstance. It comes from breathing deeply into your dreams and oxygenating your brain, just as you did as an energetic, unstoppable child. Reach back and find that joy again and make this business your great masterpiece.

Lie #

It Takes Money to Make Money

We often hear the "it takes money to make money" lie when desperate small business owners are trying to go get a big loan, or when they're going to bring in an unsavory (or overly demanding and meddlesome) character who's going to now be an investor in their business. And falling into the quicksand of the "it takes money to make money" myth, they get into even deeper trouble.

This happens because once you revive your cash flow with a big loan or investment, fresh thinking stops. The unearned money lulls you to sleep. It allows you to just stop creating.

The whole concept of succeeding versus not succeeding is a result of thinking versus not thinking. Anything that stops your thinking and gives you a vacation from creative thought and innovative ideas is going to harm your business financially. Because unearned money will muffle your drive and spirit.

If you're fat with unearned money (from loans or investments) and too full to even push away from the table, you are just not thinking anymore. You're not asking good questions. You're no longer asking, "How can we get customers in this weekend? What can we offer? How do we get customers back who came in once?" And to stop asking those questions is to stop creating a good business.

So before you believe this myth and go looking for money, ask yourself first, "What if I couldn't get any money? How would I do it?" Because in the end, those are always your best ideas. Not the ideas where you needed money to execute them. If it's going to take a lot of unearned money to accomplish, it's probably not a good idea.

Remember: This is your small business you're talking about. Not some corporate giant that needs to borrow on a large scale to manage huge leverages of inventory and labor. Many small businesses get their bad ideas from trying to emulate big business. That in itself is a bad idea.

She Was at the End of Her Rope

A woman named Cindy from Boise, Idaho, was at the end of her rope. She decided as a last-ditch effort to take a small business seminar because she just didn't know what else to do. How could she possibly save her little business? By borrowing more money? No. Something told her that the ideas in the seminar would mean more than any financial rescue would.

"The day after the seminar, I learned that I'd been evicted from my store," said Cindy. "I had to make the decision of whether or not to go on. If I hadn't just been at the seminar, I would have completely given up on it."

Cindy is a great example of choosing the most powerful of three options: (1) borrow more money, (2) go out of business, or (3) learn the truth about what works.

Soon Cindy had moved her business into a new store space with a new name, after successfully using all the seminar tools for success.

"Even though I was out of money, I was alive with ideas," said Cindy. "I had so much certainty and enthusiasm that everyone around me pitched in to help. The vendors all gave me a break because they could tell I was for real, just by the way I was speaking. I even shared a number of the seminar truths with my vendors and became like a coach to their businesses, too, and they were happy to give me credit until I got back on my feet."

Most people in Cindy's position would have taken one of the other two options. They would have either shut down, or else thrown more money into the business. That's because everyone in a struggling business seems to accept the erroneous belief that "if I could just inject enough dollars into my business, it would be successful."

But the truth is, throwing more money into the business does not save it. In fact, it makes things worse. Money may postpone the collapse, but it will also deepen the collapse. Think of giving a heroin addict a large dose of heroin as he or she passes through the final stages of a painful detox: You make him or her feel better, but the ultimate detox has just been made much worse (and the action could result in death).

You will achieve a real breakthrough once you accept this: If your business can't make it without money, it can't make it with money. So if you didn't get that loan you wanted, be grateful. It might wake you up to what really works. Necessity is the mother of reinvention.

One of the first small businesses Sam consulted with was a memorable one simply because it illustrated so dramatically that it is not money that turns things around.

A lady named Catherine from Iowa called him and told him her story, and it seemed as if her sad tale was out of a Charles Dickens novel! As she spoke about her dire condition, it just kept getting worse and worse. It was actually depressing for Sam to even have to listen to it all.

Catherine was 63 years old, single, and living in a trailer, and her income was very low from her small business of teaching six neighborhood kids piano lessons. She had no money. She realized she wouldn't ever be able to retire!

She saw our advertisement in the newspaper for a home study video course on how to improve your business. Catherine called Sam up to ask if the small business truth ideas (as outlined in this book) could work for her. At the time, the home study course was priced at about $300, and Catherine said that $300 was a huge amount of money for her. In fact, it would take pretty much all the money she had left in the bank, just to buy the course. If she bought the course, she would have no other money left to do anything for her business.

"So I told her that these ideas do work if you use them," Sam said. "I told her, however, that it was like joining a gym. You can't just join a gym and get results; you actually have to use the gym."

Sam told her that if she applied the basic truths he taught about business she would get results. But even if she didn't, all the materials and home study courses were covered by a 100-percent money-back guarantee, so if she wasn't satisfied with the course she would get all of her money back.

Catherine decided that she had no choice. She had nowhere else to turn. Her financial world was collapsing around her. The information would have to work. And therefore she made her decision.

"So I received a money order from Catherine," said Sam. "I sent her the video home study course about building her small business up, and after she received it, I called her and coached her on a couple of specific things to do. And I was a bit nervous for her, of course, because if it's all the money she has, it kind of makes you worried whether she's doing the right thing. My first advice was that she try to get her business out of the trailer and go to a local school and ask to rent rooms in the evenings in which to teach her lessons. And I told her a couple other ideas about no-cost marketing, and I shared the story about how my wife and I started our own successful business literally by handing out inexpensive photocopied flyers. And Catherine said she was going to do everything I told her to."

Two weeks later, she called Sam to update him on the situation. She had indeed approached the local private school to rent rooms, as he'd told her to. And the principal of the school listened to her request and said, "Rent? No way, you can have the space. We would love to have a piano teacher at the school to send our students to."

Look at how the fresh application of the *want to* was producing immediate results!

The school principal continued talking to Catherine. "A piano teacher here would be really convenient," he said. "You can use the space at no charge. You don't have to rent it." And then the principal said, "By the way, do you have some brochures or flyers that I could pass out to the students to tell them about how they can get lessons from you right now? We'd need about 300 to send home with all the kids."

In two weeks, Catherine had more than 40 students who were taking lessons from her at the school. (Remember that she had been down to six!) People started asking her if she knew a guitar teacher and a voice teacher. So Catherine found a guitar teacher and a voice teacher to subcontract with, and she was now making a good commission from these other teachers. This was all done with no money! These were just good ideas! Ideas plus action.

Catherine ended up increasing her income to more than $3,000 per month instantly. For her, on the brink of total poverty, that was a financial windfall. She did this without using money. She had found success by using new ideas for marketing herself and a firm commitment to make the ideas work. For the first time in her life Catherine had a powerful combination of *how to* and *want to*. Previously, she had neither.

Now, $3,000 a month may not seem like a fortune for a small business owner, but when you're barely scraping by the poverty line, it's a life-changing amount. It's also one of the many stories we receive daily that prove that you can make money without money. Fresh ideas, determination, and action: These are the only assets you need.

Learn to Create Your Own Money

Another good illustration of the fact that it does not take money to make money is Sam Beckford himself, now known throughout the United States and Canada as the "Small Business Millionaire." When Sam got down to nothing, he made some Xerox copies of fliers about his little business and just went out and pounded the pavement to find customers. He succeeded at finding them because the appeal in the flyers was just right (see Chapter 5 on how to do this), and the rest is history.

It wasn't money that did it for him, it was an idea being put into effect. Your business will succeed because of ideas and action, not because you have been well-funded.

"It was the desire to create our own money that won the day," said Sam. "So inside of your so-called limitation—the lack of money—you will find the gold: the ideas you need to make your business successful. And that is how and why you can beat your bigger, more established competitors. They don't have a reason to do the things that you're going to do. They don't have to go find fresh business ideas as you do. They can 'afford' to say, 'It's five o'clock on a

Friday, let's wrap it up. Another call from a customer? Forget it, let it go to voice mail; we don't need the business.' They can 'afford' to do that because they have this big pile of money. But history shows that this well-financed comfort zone can do them in if they don't wake up."

Sam described another reason why succeeding without money gives you a competitive advantage: "We have two competitors of our small business today that are quite big," he said. "One is a chain that has international money behind it and is run by managers. And the managers are very slack on following up and getting back to customers. So their business doesn't do nearly as well as our business does. Their definition of marketing (I know because I talked to the employees there) is radically different from our definition of marketing. They think marketing is handing out a limited number of ineffective flyers. And this is a big store with a lot of money behind it. By contrast, when we started our business, we handed out 3,000 flyers personally! And the manager of one of these stores thought an accomplishment was getting 700 flyers distributed by someone outside the company. And I was thinking, that's nothing. I mean, now we're doing in the multiple thousands of thousands, several times a year. So their money has made them complacent in that area.

"And then the other business that we see as a big competitor is a second generation family business. I find there is a lot of 'death in the comfort zone' there, too. Because the second-generation business owner has never really seen the struggle, he or she never had to wake up and say, 'We're going to do whatever it takes.' They just have the belief that it's a money tree and it's always going to produce. So if he or she wants to leave 10 minutes early, they just leave. They figure they've got enough money backed up to cover it.

"And we are outperforming both of our competitors because we do not believe that it takes money to make money. It takes fresh energy and ever-evolving customer benefits. It takes creative thinking. Unearned money gets in the way of that."

Money Just Diminishes Your *Want To*

In every successful small business there is a proper balance between the *how to* and the *want to*. An infusion of unearned money takes away too much of the *want to*. If we have a big pile of injected money and we know our business doesn't have to make a sale for the next week or month, or if we're brainwashed into the related lie that "businesses don't make a profit until their fourth year anyway," we are getting our business into even deeper trouble. Most small businesses are out of business before they can verify that fourth-year profit myth. Was it true? They'll never know, because they went out of business in their second year.

When you have unearned money covering your expenses you don't need to go out and make that sale! You don't need to say, "How can we be profitable? How can we actually make this thing give me a good salary?"

Repetition of a Bad Idea Is Not a Good Idea

Mason was a small business owner who called us and said, "I've just been putting more and more money into this business, and I am assuming some day all this investment will pay off. It will, won't it? I mean, all the times I've put my own savings in to this business, it will pay off one day, right?"

Wrong, Mason. Wrong assumption.

The very fact that you are taking money from other sources to keep your business alive means that it probably will not survive.

We encounter so many sad situations where an owner's husband is a dentist or some other type of successful businessperson, and he is feeding money to his wife's small business because "it can't survive without it."

Or, just as often, the wife has a good job and is persuaded to put a large portion of her own earnings into her husband's failing little enterprise. What finally happens is that the business turns into something that will never make money because the expectation of it making money is no longer there. You need that expectation! You need to demand of your business that it make money.

Learn to Stop Feeding the Fox

A friend of ours had a cabin out in the woods and told us about a fox that used to come around the back door of the cabin. Soon our friend started leaving food there for the fox. It was fun to do. And the fox started coming by every day to get the leftovers or whatever wonderful cooked items were being set outside.

But soon our friend realized his mistake. He finally decided to stop feeding the fox, because he realized that if the fox got dependent on the food, it would stop digging for rodents (or whatever it liked to eat). And when the day came for our friend to leave the cabin, the pet fox may have lost its survival instincts. Its claws would not be sharp, its teeth would not be sharp, and it would not be used to having to go find food. And the thing that he thought was actually helping the fox could actually be the thing that killed it.

Can you see the parallel to the husband and the wife's business? Because in the name of "helping a spouse get through," they've killed each business's survival mechanisms. You help more by not helping.

Do those little businesses need help? Yes! But not money. They need fresh ideas and fresh action plans. They need fresh *want to* and fresh *how to*. Money just postpones that. Additional money makes the situation even worse, because if you keep throwing unearned money in, the hole to dig out of gets deeper and deeper.

So don't turn your own business into that fox by believing the lie that it takes money to make money. Here is the truth you can immediately replace that lie with: You should not give your business money. Your business should give you money!

Isn't that why you opened your business to begin with? If so, then you need a business with sharp claws and teeth.

Sam failed five times to make a business work. But the business of his that made the most money, and is still making the most money, is the one that had no money to start with at all.

"We had money to start all the other businesses that we tried," said Sam, "and we had none for the one business that was ultimately successful. That one succeeded because we had something more important than money—we had the knowledge of how to continuously add value to our customers, how to selectively choose great customers, how to make a profit, and then how to duplicate that process over and over."

Before starting that successful business, Sam was down to $50 worth of photocopies and no money.

"I remember we made 1,000 copies, and it was five cents a copy," said Sam. "And we cut those pages into three pieces, so it was three pieces per 8 1/2 × 11 page, so we went to 3,000 houses and distributed those flyers. And it was tough, because we walked to every single house. And that's how we actually started our business, and that was the beginning of the business that made us millionaires. And we took the profits that we made from those 3,000 flyers and we put that into more marketing that worked, and everything we did in that business was done under the idea that what we do in this business has to work. It has to pay off. It has to be accountable. If we would have had $100,000 to start that business, we may never have made it. Because we would not have learned the basic advertising principles (samples in Chapter 5 and on *www.smallbusinesstruth.com*) that gave us customers."

With extra unearned money in hand, people do many ineffective things in the name of advertising. A small business will stick an ad on the side of a bus somewhere and if doesn't work they say, "Oh well, it's only a couple of thousand dollars, who cares? We've got lots more of that left!"

If you don't have that requirement for things such as marketing expenses to work, they won't. When there's no such expectation, you're not really paying attention. It's not that important to you because you can think, "Why spend that much time thinking about this flyer? If it doesn't work, it's not going to make a difference anyway."

But everything needed to work for Sam, so he was just down to one last mission: learn how things work. Learn how businesses succeed. He had no where else to go but there.

Living in the Profitable Now

Your business exists to make a profit, and that's what it has to do. Therefore you figure out how to manage your time accordingly. You manage your time according to what's profitable and what's not.

Many business owners thinking they need a loan also say that their biggest problem is time management, as if these two problems were unrelated! They haven't realized yet that the best time-management system they could ever use is for them to expect to profit from every activity they do.

You can do this. As you plan and then create your day, you can have your activities actually be profitable. All of them. But you must evaluate the tasks you plan to do based on one vital truth-seeking question: "Is this something that's going to help make more profit for the business or not?"

If it's not, don't do it! Have someone else do it. It's your business, so it's not efficient for you to be doing the work of a $10-per-hour person. Even if it needs to be done! Get someone to do it. This is your masterpiece, not your prison.

Yes, you do want to "lead from the front" and be out there with customers, but not just to cover for someone who called in sick. You are there to gather valuable information from customers about what drew them into your business and what it takes to thrill them so that they will refer others.

Ask this question about all your daily efforts: Is this something that leads me to greater profit? Because then there will be a lot less taking of coffee breaks and reading the paper, and talking about endless personal matters with employees when you could be doing activities to advance the profitability of your business. There will also be a lot less of you, the owner, stepping in to do minimum-wage activity at your business. A total misuse of your brainpower and energy!

Ask yourself to always be aware of two levels of consciousness in yourself. The lower level is just that mindless level of working inside your business and being very busy. But the higher-consciousness level is the creative level of working on your business, to make it make you more money. Are you doing something of high-return value or just doing something?

Most business owners operate at the lower, "just being busy" level of consciousness all day long. Day in, day out, he or she shows up and tries to work "harder" but doesn't seem to be getting anywhere. They suffer from the delusion that they are "working really hard!" But if it's just low-consciousness activity they're doing all day, they are eventually going to go out of business.

So respect your mental energy, and keep noticing where it gets invested. Make your business make you money.

Force it to. Don't fall for the "it takes money to make money" small business lie. Even though you will hear it constantly from others. We've all seen the real truth: Small businesses that are very well-financed are usually failing miserably.

In fact, the businesses that were the most well-financed in all of American history failed the most miserably! Those were the "dot-com" businesses. They literally had billions and billions of dollars. So, if it just took money to make money, those people should now have, in theory, more money than anyone has ever made. However, most of those dot-com companies went bankrupt because they didn't acquire the vital knowledge of how to get customers, keep customers, and inspire customers to keep coming back.

And it makes no difference what industry you're in, either. No type of business is uniquely dependent on big money bailing them out. If you are reading this saying, "Well, my industry's different," you are wrong. The bottom line is that every business needs to know the truth about how to get and keep customers without outside money and it doesn't matter what business you're in.

Your strategy for getting and keeping customers, once it's in place, will be much more powerful than money. So let's read on and discover some proven strategies to do that!

Lie # 3

We Just Need to Get Our Name Out There

Again and again you hear people tell you that you need to get your name out there. Advertising reps will tell you that name recognition is vital, and your ad *must get your name out there* over and over again.

Not true! Your ad doesn't need to get your name out. Your ad needs to *get your customer in.*

Your business needs an ad that works to attract the exact type of customer that you want to sell to, and keep selling to. The purpose of advertising is not to "build awareness" or "increase your name ID." The purpose of your advertising is to create a sale!

So watch out: There is a lot of bad information floating around about advertising.

And "bad information" is just a nice way of putting it. When your friendly local newspaper ad rep tries to tell you that your small business needs some name recognition, and that the most important thing you can do is to "get the word out," then you have just been told a lie.

This lie is not unique to newspaper reps. All media reps, billboard reps, radio ad reps—anyone at all pitching "awareness" is steering you toward failure.

Because there is absolutely no value to your business whatsoever in having a lot of people simply know your business's name. That lie has cost more small businesses more unnecessary wasteful expense than any other we can think of.

To make advertising really pay off for you, you need to understand what advertising is! Advertising is "salesmanship in print." And that hasn't changed since the former Canadian policeman (turned advertising genius) John E. Kennedy changed the face of advertising forever with those three words in 1905.

So think of your ad as a salesperson. Make it *be* a salesperson. Would your salesperson get a sale by contacting your prospective customers and just saying the company name over and over? Calling them on the phone, whispering your business's name, and hanging up?

You expect a lot more than that from a salesperson, and so you should expect a lot more than that from your advertising as well.

Make Your Ad Attract Someone

Even before you design an ad or a flyer, you may want to ask: Who are we trying to attract? What type of customer do we really want? (The same kind of talk you would have with a salesperson before sending him or her out into the world to make a sale.) Do we want a customer that will be profitable for our business? Or, do we want cheapskate price shoppers?

One of the most important small business truths we could ever pass on to you is that the quality of your business is directly related to the quality of your customer. To make your business successful, you need customers who are good, solid citizens, customers who will be with you for a long time. And your advertising is a great place to start building that kind of customer base.

A Recipe for Business Misery

If you pick up your local newspaper and look at ads for small businesses you will see a common pattern in how the ads are designed. Look right now in your paper to see if this isn't the way it is:

1. Business name at the top of the ad.
2. A discount offer, such as 20 percent off a certain product or service, or an el cheapo price-related offer ($19.95 oil change).
3. The phone number and address at the bottom of the ad.

This common type of advertising is not salesmanship. It's closer to a bulletin board listing in a dormitory lobby. It's crude and brutally brief. It has no chance to start the sales process toward a nice high-profit sale for you. It does little more than "get your name out" and establish you as a low-price (and probably low-value) business. If this ad even accomplishes these limited objectives, it is still not helping you in the long run. Because in the long run you want to grow a highly profitable business, and that starts with the first ad you place.

So don't use this bare-bones kind of advertising! Just don't. Because you are wasting money and attracting the wrong type of customers (that is, if you are attracting customers at all).

Here are two typical ads we just saw in our own local paper:

Walnut Creek Equipment Inc.
Outdoor Power Equipment
Ask Santa for a STIHL!
Save on the MS 170 Chainsaw
just $299.00!
While supplies last!
2610 Powder Keg Drive
555-2345

> **Lube Master**
> Winter Special
> Oil Change $19.95
> Expires December 31
> 536 Saddle Street
> Mon-Sat 9-6
> 555-1234

Look at your own local paper and you'll see ads very similar to these. In fact, you may even be running one yourself. And if you are running one yourself, you will be able to verify that it doesn't work. Even though your rep is now telling you that you need to be patient. It's all about "repetition." But it's not. If your ad doesn't work, it doesn't work. It doesn't matter how many times you repeat it.

If you have the wrong combination to a lock, your chances of opening the lock do not increase each time you try it. If you are dialing the wrong phone number, it doesn't help you to dial it many more times in your attempt to reach someone.

Your ad is there to reach someone. It must reach someone. If it doesn't reach someone the very first time, it is a waste of money.

Many newspaper reps will tell you that you have to run your ad 10 times to get "frequency." Your rep will insist, "If people see it enough, they will respond." Knowingly or not, your rep is lying.

Time will pass. You'll be getting no response to your ad. And now that you and your rep both realize that the ad is not working, your rep may then tell you to make the same ad bigger, so more people will notice it. "Don't change the copy, just make the bad ad bigger!" (That's the same as a waiter saying: "Don't like the pie? Why don't you try a bigger piece!")

Frequency and size sound like logical reasons people respond to advertising, but they are both false. Frequency in and of itself doesn't make any difference. Neither does size. Not if the ad is ineffective.

There is a restaurant somewhere in your city that you have driven by at least twice a day for over a year now. You keep seeing the name, and the restaurant doesn't look at all unpleasant. You've probably seen their sign more than 1,000 times! But you have never eaten there. Frequency and knowing about the restaurant are not enough. A bigger sign on the restaurant won't help either. If you don't have a reason to go, you don't have a reason to go.

From Broadway to the Right Way

Frank Mastercola and his wife, of Park Ridge, New Jersey, were clients of ours a while back when their small business was doing okay, but not thriving. Frank and his wife were former Broadway performers and had acted in shows such as *Cats* and *Starlight Express*. They had worked with Bob Fosse, Michael Bennett, Cheeta Rivera, Liza Minelli, and other noteworthy professionals in the industry.

After their success on Broadway, Frank's wife, Anita, opened a small studio business. She started teaching music and dance, and four years later Frank decided to join her and get more involved in running the studio.

"Our student total was in the 400s for about three years," Frank told us. "And our original advertising philosophy was that *getting the word out* is the best way to sell your school. But it turns out you can't just rely on that. And that's why we were just spinning our wheels. So you came along with your advertising system at the perfect time for us and we thought, 'Of course!'"

By simply switching from the "getting your name out there" falsehood to the small business *truth* that advertising is salesmanship, Frank and Anita increased their student base to 800! Twice their original business! They are now looking forward to purchasing a new building for their school.

So let's go deeper into the two ads we cited earlier, to see exactly the kinds of changes *you* can make to increase your business the way Frank and Anita did.

Question: What type of customer will the Lube Master ad attract? Look again:

Lube Master
Winter Special
Oil Change $19.95
Expires December 31
536 Saddle Street
Mon-Sat 9-6
555-1234

Answer: Someone looking for a cheap oil change, right?

This ad is trying the old "loss leader" strategy. Get a customer to buy something cheap to get them in the door. But this ad probably won't attract much response. Cheap oil changes are everywhere, aren't they? There's nothing compelling here. Nothing special. Therefore, no sale is being made. Remember: For an ad to work for you, it must be *salesmanship in print.*

But even if this ad actually gets a response, you will have attracted a price shopper. Someone motivated by price. And then you will have the impossible task of getting them to come back and pay regular price for future services. Good luck.

Try to upgrade a price shopper into a value buyer and both you and the customer end up frustrated, angry, and betrayed. Businesses do this all the time when they attract the wrong customers to begin with and then try to change them to a good high-value customer.

You must change the belief behind your ad and the belief behind your business. What you believe about your business is what your customer will believe about your business. It has to start with you.

People can get their oil changed anywhere. A cheap oil change is nothing special.

So, you might ask, what *is* special? What *does* someone with a car want more than just a cheap oil change?

There are two answers we know about for sure: (1) time and (2) convenience!

Remember this: *Time is the new money.*

According to the latest income surveys, 20 percent of the population controls 47 percent of the disposable income.

That means one out of five people have so much money to buy things with, that, relatively speaking, they're not concerned about the price at all. Does it make sense to focus your ad's message on something that doesn't concern them?

Because those 20 percent are your ideal customers! Money is not the main factor in their decision to shop with you. You are. You are the main factor in their decision, and that's how you want it to be. Your quality, your service, your commitment to them. That's where you want it to be, because that's where you profit margin is, and that's where your data base of lifelong customers comes from. Not from one-time price shoppers.

So, here's an ad that reinvents the cheap oil change and attracts a totally different customer:

Too Busy to Change Your Oil?
We'll pick your car up, change the oil, and we'll clean it and drop it off to your home or office with your favorite Starbucks beverage!
Lube Master—Executive Valet
555-2345

Who will this ad attract? Someone who is more concerned about time than money. Someone who loses more money per minute hanging around an oil change joint than all the attendants earn combined. Someone who sees the time spent waiting for his or her car as billable hours down the drain. Someone who wants to golf or play with his or her kids on the weekend, rather than running errands. That's your ideal customer!

Always Use the High-Value Customer Ad Formula

Here is the simple advertising formula that helped make Sam Beckford a millionaire:

STEP 1: Place a headline at the top of the ad that solves a problem or gives a unique benefit that is more valuable than just the product. Your name should never be at the top of an ad, because it does nothing to attract customers. People don't care what your business name is. They care about what your business can do for them.

STEP 2: Make no reference to price in the ad.

If price is your only selling feature you are in a losing battle. Remember that one in five consumers don't need to fret about price. We have all bought things that were expensive but worth it. Price is just a detail, not the deal itself.

STEP 3: Offer a unique service (that only you provide) as the "hook," not a lowball price. People buy for many reasons other than price. Once you believe this you will attract customers that will continue to prove it to you and verify your belief. Higher-value customers who like your unique offer are the ones who stay with you. Remember that the two car brands with the highest repeat-purchase rates are Lexus and Cadillac! Is that because of the price?

Let's use our small business truth formula (see *www.smallbusinesstruth.com*) to reinvent the second ad, the one about the chainsaw. Here is the original:

Walnut Creek Equipment Inc.

Outdoor Power Equipment

Ask Santa for a STIHL!

Save on the MS 170 Chainsaw
just $299.00!

While supplies last

2610 Powder Keg Drive

555-2345

First ask yourself, "Who will buy a $300 chainsaw as a Christmas gift?" Answer: The wife of a man who likes the outdoors. Try to remember that gift purchases are not made by the recipient of the gift! (That sounds obvious, as if we didn't need to tell you that. But during the holiday season, look at how many ads are thoughtlessly misdirected. Remember: Your ad is doing a sales job for you. Make it talk to the *buyer*.)

The majority of wives who will spend $300 on a chainsaw for a gift are not price-conscious shoppers. If they were, they would be looking at $39 wrench sets, not $300 chainsaws.

Question number two: Would most wives like to go to a power equipment store and spend time looking at chainsaws? Probably not. They would be intimidated at the very thought.

So, taking those observations into account, here's our reinvented ad that attracts the ideal customer for the chainsaw gift:

**The Perfect Gift for the
Outdoorsman Husband**

We'll deliver
a boxed, fully gift-wrapped
STIHL MS 170 Chainsaw
and put it under your tree.
Or we'll help you hide it until
the big day
to keep the surprise.
We'll even drop off
a 2-foot tester log
so he can try it out right away!
With our "he'll love it"
guarantee let him try it out
and if he isn't thrilled
we'll pick it up
and let him exchange it for any
other model he wants.

Walnut Creek Equipment
555-1234

How much is the chainsaw? Could it be $50 more than the first ad? Who cares? It's worth it. We are no longer selling a chainsaw, we are now selling an event! The log in the backyard to try it out, the hiding the box, not having to lug it through a store. Not having to worry whether he likes it.

You have (1) spoken to the buyer, (2) painted a picture of a great Christmas day, and (3) even helped to keep the surprise. You are a hero to your customer. You have solved her biggest problems with your ad!

Remember: One in five people walking around in your community don't need to be concerned with price. They will buy something because they feel like it and they will gladly pay extra to have a great event and experience. Everyone wants to splurge on events such as weddings, anniversaries, and Christmas.

But that all sounds like a lot of work!

Isn't it extra work to wrap and deliver a chainsaw? Yes, of course. Most businesses owners would not do this because of that. That could be your advantage over them.

Because this *little bit* of extra work you do up front will save you from the *endless* work of keeping a struggling business alive. It will put you on the path to prosperity, a path that will lead you to lots of vacation time, and happy profitable years ahead.

And once you get the hang of it you'll find out something additionally rewarding: Working to get paid well by pleasant customers does not feel like work. It feels like you are finally executing a fine craft. It feels like mastery. Because it is.

High-profit customers mean a high-profit business. You can't separate them. If you want, really want, higher profits, then the market is wide open. One in five people are waiting to have their problems solved in exchange for money. You can be the solution and reap the reward. We've trained hundreds and hundreds of small business owners just like you to learn this approach. It works for them, and it will work for you. Their stories are on our Website, so enjoy them and let yourself see the truth of this.

(You can see more unique high-value customer ads for six different businesses and get free reports on further strong systems of newspaper advertising at *www.smallbusinesstruth.com*.)

There is nothing mysterious about advertising. It either works for you or it doesn't. If your advertising is not working (or cannot be measured), stop spending money on it. Demand that it delivers a measurable return on your investment. Hold your advertising as accountable as you would any other salesperson, because that's what it is.

Lie # 4

Experience Will Benefit Me

We've all heard it said that "experience is the best teacher," but ask the woman who has just married her third alcoholic husband whether that's true.

Some people have had a lot of "experience" living with people using drugs and alcohol, but that does not make them better at it. Usually, it makes them worse.

If your doctor tells you, after looking at your heart, that you need to quit smoking, it probably would not occur to you to offer this objection: "Don't worry, Doc, I've had a lot of experience smoking."

Because once again, the experience is not beneficial to you. In fact, it harms you.

In business, the same thing holds true. If your experience is experience doing things the ineffective way, then your experience is doing you more harm than good. Totally inexperienced competitors that knew how to effectively advertise and effectively serve customers could outperform your business right from the beginning, even if they had no experience whatsoever.

Your experience can put you into a rut that has you failing at key elements in your business time and time again. And the difference between a rut and a grave is just a few feet.

If Thomas Edison (who tried to invent the lightbulb ten thousand times before it worked) had repeated the same experiment every single time, and not changed anything, he could have said, "In my experience, the lightbulb can not work." That's how most people fail to invent a profitable business.

They keep repeating what doesn't work.

Most people believe that if they hang in there long enough, experience alone will improve their ability to make their business work. And that is simply not the truth.

Deanna and Aaron started a small sales training company 12 years ago thinking that Deanna's ability as a public speaker and Aaron's accounting skills would be a perfect combination for success. After a few years of losing money and being burdened with big debts to vendors, they hired a business consultant we know named Rolf.

"What is your current strategy for turning this thing around?" the consultant Rolf asked during his first week on the job.

"Strategy?" said Aaron.

"Yes. Your current plan. Let's look at that plan, and see where we can deconstruct it and put it back together so that it works faster for you," said Rolf.

"What plan are you referring to?" Deanna asked.

"Your success plan," said the coach. "Your turnaround strategy."

"Well, we don't really know what you mean," said Aaron. "We're just kind of trying to fight fires around here. We've both taken huge pay cuts, and our vendors have met with us to give us some more time to work things out. And we just assumed…."

"You see, we have faith," Deanna interrupted. "We pray a lot together, and we have faith that if we stay the course, and don't lose that faith, things will turn around, eventually, through experience. I mean, it stands to reason that if you do something long enough you'll get pretty good at it, right?"

"No, that's not right," their consultant said. "It *doesn't* stand to reason. Because if you are on the wrong road to town it doesn't matter how long you stay on that road, it won't get you into town. It doesn't even matter if you pray or have faith in that road. The wrong road is the wrong road."

"That's not what everyone tells us," said Deanna. "Everyone tells you from the minute you start your business that it's all about hard work and experience. It's just common sense that the longer and harder you work at something the better you get."

"Common sense is wrong about that," said the coach. "Look at your own numbers. Those numbers aren't lying. They're the only truth you've got right now. Numbers don't know how to lie. You do, but your numbers don't. You are on the wrong road to town. And not only will this road not get you into town, the longer you stay on it, the further away it will take you. So in that sense, experience and working hard are actually contributing to your failure."

Deanna and Aaron stared at each other. This was going against everything they had ever heard about life and business.

Their consultant proceeded to formulate a new plan for them based on the principles in this book. The execution of the plan took six months, but the company finally became profitable. And a year after that they were much more than profitable, and both Aaron and Deanna were among the most highly paid people in their community. Their own business was paying them handsomely.

"Thanks for what you have done for our business," they told their consultant.

"That's what a business is for," he reminded them. "It exists to pay you. It does not exist to make you miserable."

After 5 Business Failures: Success!

If you value and perpetuate experience alone, that very experience can deepen and solidify the dysfunctional business behaviors that are keeping you from the windfall profits that were the original goals of your business.

Be wary of the value of experience. Even experience that other people have. If you listen to negative people just because they have experience, you may become infected with the same small business lies that they are infected with. Failure can be contagious. Value *success* in others. Not experience.

Many people with "experience" have told our seminar clients that our principles are too simple and that the success stories we have built with our client base are simply "too good to be true."

Well, they got two things right. The results are "good" and the case histories are "true," starting with Sam Beckford's own case history. Sam became a millionaire with his small business (after failing at five others) by finally applying these simple truths himself. This book is exactly how he did it.

Some people think becoming a millionaire the way Sam did is a dream concept. They see it as an over-the-rainbow goal, similar to winning the lottery.

But is that really what becoming a millionaire is? There are literally millions of people in the United States and Canada—not thousands, but millions—who have become millionaires by running small businesses just like yours. So the odds are actually good that you can, too. But you have to begin by being honest—not blue-sky optimistic—just honest about your very real opportunity to have your business make you rich.

Finding Your Own Road to Freedom

Chris Napoli, of Philadelphia, attended our seminars in Vancouver. Based on what he learned, he changed the way he was doing business. He later reported back to us that his "personal and business life have changed dramatically" since implementing some of the ideas we teach.

"As far as my business," Chris told us, "I don't have to work in my business anymore. Sometimes there are months that go by when I have tons of free time. And because I have so much free time, I get to focus on the high leverage activities that pay off exponentially. Two years ago, I was working between 60 and 80 hours on certain weeks. And now there are certain months that go by where I may not work at all for two weeks."

Chris Napoli learned that it's not hard work and experience that makes for success, *it's doing what works.*

There are aspects of your own business that can start making money for you the same way, once you get the nine falsehoods completely out of your system and put the simple truths into play.

Chris had originally thought that if he hung in there long enough with his old ways of doing business, experience alone, all by itself, would see him through. But it just wasn't happening. When he attended the seminars he saw that he was on the wrong road with his advertising, with his employee relations, with his pricing structure, and with almost every other aspect of his business. Chris thought he had been following the dictates of "common sense," told to him by other people who either had no businesses of their own, or were failing in them.

Failure is common. Four out of five small businesses fail. And that's where most of the "common sense" is coming from: the people in those struggling businesses. They talk. They complain. They confirm each other's worst fears. The other 20 percent aren't talking to you because they're too busy off on some vacation island enjoying the fruits of their success.

You must begin your own turnaround plan by not looking to experience alone to show you what to do. Experience won't show you much of anything. Experience is just accumulated time, and what's the inherent value in that?

One of the things people always tell you growing up is that "practice makes perfect." Well, practice *doesn't* make perfect if you're practicing the wrong thing; it just reinforces the wrong way to do it. To succeed in business, you need to WAKE UP! Wake up to what works. What works is not a secret! It's not some intangible quality some people have and some people don't. You can learn to be successful in your business. It is teachable and learnable, and there's nothing mysterious about it at all.

That's a vital factor in your deciding to succeed. You must realize that if there are literally millions of millionaires, then the way to do it can't be all that mysterious. But here's what stops most people: They personalize their failures. The minute their business gets frustrating, they wonder about their personal worth: Do I have what it takes? People are soon making up all kinds of wild, untrue things about successful people. They think they have strange, unusual willpower and drive. They think they are lucky and connected. They think things that drive them deeper into low energy and low self-esteem.

Do not make up negative things about yourself if your business is struggling. It is not about you and your qualities. It is about your choices and level of understanding. Once you reach a new level of understanding about how businesses succeed, your business will also succeed. No matter who you are and what your genetics are and how your parents treated you. You can do this. But, you must choose to do it. You must decide to commit to it, and raise your level of consciousness and understanding, or it won't happen.

What you will find if you focus your consciousness on success long enough, is the truth about how to make your business work for *you*. So that you aren't working for *it*. The truth is, the things you can do to make your business succeed, *you can do right now,* no matter what level of experience you have. This can be your very first day in your new business, and you can do all the right things to make your business succeed.

Lie # 5

Lowering Prices Boosts Business

Low prices do not boost business at all. In fact, low prices can cost you your business.

Sally started a dry cleaning business near Sam's business in Vancouver. She started optimistically because the plaza was in the middle of a fast-growing, upscale suburb. Her business began with a small surge, but then her customers became scarce.

Sam took his dry cleaning to Sally because it was convenient to where his own business was located, and he would chat a bit with her about business. Soon Sally began to ask Sam for ideas on what to do to get more business. He mentioned a couple of things that we teach at our Small Business Truth Website, such as following up with customers and adding on extra services, and he suggested maybe a free pick-up and drop-off service for her business if someone requested more than a certain amount of cleaning. All things that would allow her to strengthen her pricing structure.

"Because she was just sitting around waiting for customers, I figured she had time to drive around and do those extra services," Sam reasoned.

Sam also suggested Sally approach stores in the local mall that sold high-end women's and men's clothing and offer them a free first cleaning with the purchase of a suit. If people were going to buy an expensive suit or dress, they probably would want an upper-end cleaner, so why not target that market? Sam was trying to lead Sally to the truth about successful business: Success comes from good, repeat customers and strong, profit-producing prices.

But this will not turn out to be a success story.

This story about Sam and Sally has no happy ending, because although Sally listened to the ideas politely, she never followed up on any of them. Instead, she made a fateful bad decision that eventually would drive her out of business.

She decided to try to boost business by lowering prices even more than her already under-market position and offering some two-for-one specials on shirts and suits. She also invested in a window artist who painted huge, garish "LOWEST PRICES IN TOWN" lettering on her windows. About three disastrous months later she confided to Sam, in a weary voice, "You just can't make any real money in the dry cleaning business; the overhead is too high, the labor is too expensive, and people only want the cheapest prices."

It was ironic that she felt that way, because in that same year, in the local paper's business section an article came out talking about the unusually high profits some people were making in the dry cleaning industry! The article revealed the story behind how this "sleeper" industry had become a source of great wealth for some of its owners.

Would things have been different if Sally had realized that the industry was a sleeper success? Not really. Because Sally could have seen 10 articles similar to that, and they wouldn't have mattered to her. She was convinced that in her dry cleaning business it was impossible to make money unless she offered dramatic price incentives. She was convinced.

Sally was one of many victims of the myth that lowering your prices is a good way to stimulate business. Some of these victims even believe it's their only option when times are tough. It's too bad people fall for that one, because it is simply not true that your customer is only responding to your price.

Your Fear Is Not the Customer's Fear

The biggest fear that most of us have when we start our business is that we might not make it. Because we all hear the statistics that say 80 percent of businesses fail in the first five years. We also hear all the other things that people tell us about small business: "It's risky; you're going to lose your shirt. Oh, don't do it, you don't want to go for some unproven thing, why don't you stay with your secure job?"

The minute we start our small business we are vulner-able to these money fears. It's not hard to slide unconsciously into a scarcity mentality. Soon we're afraid we may never have enough money.

And as we do with all other beliefs we hold, we start projecting this belief out into our external world. Now we're even projecting it on our customers. "Look at them! They have money issues! They're scared of spending!"

As Sally did, we begin to assume that the only reason the customer is not buying from us is because our prices aren't attractive enough. All these conclusions are fear-based and false.

The great American philosopher Henry David Thoreau used to say, "We don't see things as they are. We see things as *we* are."

We were attending a business Internet forum recently and a small business manager was talking about how his business was struggling, "just like the overall economy." He had convinced himself (erroneously) that his business was down as a result of the poor economy, and he had then reasoned from that position: "The reason I don't have money in my business is only because people out there, my customers, don't have money. So the solution to that is for me to keep prices low, to address their shortage."

That man was heading in the wrong direction. He had quickly bought in to small business lie number five, and it was leading him to disaster.

Let's not project our own struggle onto the customer! It compounds the error. The customer is *not* struggling with paying our price. We just think so. Somehow we have to learn to get this truth and get it down deep in our soul that *lower prices are not the answer.*

When Harry and Sasha started their own successful business running a little print shop, Sasha couldn't shake her childhood memories of scarcity.

"Sasha's father was a miner in a very poor part of Pennsylvania," Harry told us. "And he didn't make any money. When she was a child, her parents had no money and people around had no money, and now we live in one of the most affluent areas in the country, in a suburb of Pittsburgh you know, and there's a lot of people with a lot of money out here. But for years, in our own business, when we would want to raise prices, a lot of the reasoning for Sasha not wanting to raise the price would be because what she experienced as a child. And she would have a real guilt factor attached to raising prices. 'Oh, but I can't do that to them. After all, these customers are so loyal to me, how could I do that to them? They can't really afford it.'"

But Harry knew better. And he kept pushing their prices higher and higher to stronger levels for his business. And in the end, their customers proved that they *could* afford it. In fact, the customers were *glad* to pay solid prices for that one small, but important, printing need in their lives.

Small business truth: *People afford what they want to afford.*

We've all seen the trailer park with expensive pick-up trucks and SUVs parked there, because people will always spend money on whatever their priority is. People buy *what they want* and will pay whatever that costs. The trick is not to give them something they can afford, it's to give them something they *want*.

For you, as a business owner, it's a matter of changing your focus. Focus on what your customer wants. Then focus on what you can add to that, to address a further and deeper want. That will keep your prices climbing right along with your value to the customer.

And the good news is that once you convert from the *low price focus* to the *strong price focus*, your business will thrive! The truth that people pay for *what they want* will be proven to you. And the truth will set you free.

Raise Both Price and Value Together

Sam Beckford has become a small business millionaire by being willing to raise prices over and over again. "We don't do what I call the 'scaredy-cat raise,'" Sam explained. "That's when a price increase is so small that no one would even notice it anyway."

When Sam raises prices he raises them at least 11–15 percent.

"But we don't just raise prices, we *increase value* at the same time," Sam explained.

Increasing value helps you and your customer make a happy, confident adjustment to your new price. There are always ways you can raise value, and, in fact, if your business is to thrive, you must continuously add value to your customer. So, "How can we raise the value of what we deliver?" ought to be a daily inquiry. It can be an exciting, ongoing intellectual challenge for you and your people.

Don't try to run a business while letting your mind go to sleep on this issue. Often, if you give in to money fears, your heart overrules your mind. The louder your heart pounds the harder it is to hear yourself think. But thinking about adding value is always the answer.

You can keep your creative thinking alive by challenging yourself and your people to always think of ways to increase value to your customer. Have it be a weekly contest. Keep a suggestion box. Hold meetings about it. Because in the end, increasing value makes your price increases logical and easy to execute.

When you're increasing value, one of the first helpful hints we give clients is to first *spend money on what people can see*, not on what they can't. So when you increase your fees, always try to put some money into some improvement that people will notice. Your customers should walk away saying, "Wow, this place looks great. You improved this area, you did that upgrade." And it's just like those real estate makeover shows on TV where they take $1,000 and work two days and the house looks as if a $50,000 interior designer was there! You can do that in your business!

Additionally, you can improve the look of what you sell, and you can improve the look of your communication pieces.

You can also do *invisible* things that enhance value to your customer and that can justify a price increase. For example, if your employees are dedicated to innovative, continuous improvement, they are going to be better at the service they deliver than they were a year ago. Everybody admits it: "I deliver the product better, I have better people, I know what I'm doing more, I provide better service than I used to, simply because I've been improving over the past year."

So even if you don't do a great deal overtly, you are still providing more value than you were a year ago just by the fact that you've learned a lot about your customers' wants. That spells value to the customer.

This, by the way, is different than the "experience lie" we talked about earlier that says experience itself is enough to run your business better. It's not. You must grow in consciousness. You must make your experience be about raising value. When you stay alert to raising value, you'll always get better at serving the customer. And then charge accordingly. (If you don't, they won't appreciate the value.)

Everyone Associates Price With Value

The final irony of business lie number five: Raising prices itself will make you worth more to the customer. Customers know they get what they pay for. Blind tests show that people enjoy the taste of expensive wines more even if the testers have put the same wine in both bottles. This is not to encourage you to fool the customer, or raise your price for no reason, but it does show that you value something according to what you pay for it.

And there's another reason to raise your prices. Raising your prices raises the bar. By doing so you'll put a new obligation on yourself to make sure you're now serving

the customer better than before. Raising prices w
up. When you stay with the same low prices, you
lieve your customers like it, but you are putting your creativity to sleep in the process. Low prices put yourself and
your customer to sleep. You don't look for ways to enhance the buying experience because you're resentful at
only getting a low price for the service. Your low price
causes you to dismiss and dislike your customers because
you know subconsciously that they aren't paying a true
price for their service. Perhaps you were tempted to put
that extra touch of service on a recent job by driving it out
and delivering it yourself, but you stopped when you
thought, "At this price? No way am I going to go the extra
mile. They are getting much more than they paid for already."

The lower your prices, the more you resent your customer. Soon you're doing little passive-aggressive things
to under serve them. How dare they call me on the
phone…at the prices they are paying me? I'm not return-
ing that call.

Customers are the source of all your wealth. Sinking
into an adversarial relationship with them is fatal. It will
kill the golden goose.

Time Is More Important Than Money

Let's look at two butcher shops about 10 minutes away
from our business. They're actually across the street from
each other, on different corners, in different plazas. They
were getting along well enough until a big grocery store
with a meat department opened in a plaza down the street.

One butcher shop was owned by a woman named Jeanne. (We say "*was* owned" because the butcher shop is closed now. It shut down about two years ago and there's a Chinese restaurant where it used to be.) We used to go to Jeanne's butcher shop before it shut down. It looked the way you'd expect a butcher shop to look. It had signs crowding the front window saying, "Pot roast on sale this week!" and "Corned beef is on special!" When the big grocery store opened down the street from Jeanne's, *her prices got even lower* and soon a sign went up in her window that said, "Best prices! Best service!" in an effort to compete with the big grocery store.

Pricing was all that people cared about. Or, at least, that's what Jeanne thought. And that was the way her clerks in the store began to feel, too. In fact, her workers all talked that way when you were in there: "People want to pay less. People just price shop." (Funny how a lie repeated often enough becomes everyone's truth.)

Now, Frank's butcher store (across the street from Jeanne's) was also in the business of selling meat. And the same big threatening new grocery store was down the street from Frank, too. But unlike Jeanne, Frank is still in business.

Even though every weekend, in the Sunday newspaper, there were big grocery store coupons for meat at the cheapest prices, Frank would not panic and respond as Jeanne did. Frank's store was not caught up in the lie about price. In fact, Frank's store made no mention of having "the best" prices. Frank's store, instead, became notoriously *more* expensive than the grocery store and Jeanne's store combined!

But consider Frank's store. Stop by any day of the week, and it's packed.

The reason for this is that Frank doesn't just sell meat; he sells precut, marinated steaks, chicken, shish kabobs, and fish fillets, ready to put on the barbecue or in the oven. If you bought your meat at Jeanne's or at the grocery store, you'd save a few dollars, but you'd have to marinate your steak or chicken overnight. And who has time for that?

Frank's ready-to-go butcher shop charges premium prices and even has money left over to give away a free barbecue each year. Frank's business is thriving because he found a way to raise prices and raise value.

Jeanne is out of business because she thought lower prices were what customers would respond to.

But Jeanne's customers weren't the cheapskates she thought they were. That's why the lure of saving a few dollars didn't attract them after all. She assumed they were broke, because she was broke. But they were only broke in terms of time. And the store that was able to give them their time back (Frank's store) solved a problem for them. That's why the customers were not patrons of the low-priced supermarket a few minutes away.

Unfortunately for her, Jeanne assumed that *what's cheapest?* was the most important thing on her customer's mind. But one casual look in the typical American freezer would have revealed to Jeanne many high-priced TV dinners and frozen snacks that are bought to save time, not money. That look in the freezer would have given her the secret truth she needed: *Time is the new money.*

If You Can Save People Time, You Can Charge People Money

This summer Sam Beckford hosted a barbecue at his home for the employees who work in his company.

"I remember it was a busy time in the summer and I was at the business working late," explained Sam. "I still had to get the meat for the barbecue, and so I stopped by Frank's store. As I was walking out of the store, I realized I had spent a lot of money, but I was happy. Frank's prepped meats had saved me hours of time. All I had to do when I got back to my house was put the prepared meats directly on the barbecue. I realized that if I had gone to the grocery store, I might have paid half as much, but there's no way I would have been ready in time for the important event. And now I go back to Frank's 'expensive' store over and over again, any time we have company or are too time-strapped to cook. The time is more valuable to us than the money."

Your own customers are in the same situation, or some version of it. In the 1950s the average American household spent two hours preparing a meal. Today, the average American household spends less than thirty minutes preparing a meal! That's a startling trend that applies across the board to every type of business, including yours.

For you, time *is* money. Anything you can do to make things more convenient for your customer, and to respect your customer's time, will allow you to raise your prices. Time is really very valuable to them. Think in terms of your customers' time instead of their money, and your profits will start to increase immediately (as long as you also raise your prices accordingly.)

"When we started our business, we were actually on the lower end of the pricing spectrum," recalled Sam. "We made the classic mistake that many business owners make. We thought, 'Well, we're not really that good, we don't have that much experience, so we're going to open our business and we're going to see what everyone else is charging, and we're going to charge a little bit less. Because, you know, we haven't paid our dues, we don't have the experience, we haven't been around as long as the others have.'"

But the problem with that low price positioning is that businesses get stuck in that cheap format. It becomes a part of their identity and it deepens their fear of ever being more expensive than someone else. They have come to believe, really believe, that the only reason someone is choosing them is because they're a little less expensive!

Learning to Eliminate the Fear Factor

When we asked our coaching client Melinda to consider raising her consulting fees (she was a healthcare business consultant, and a very good one) she said she couldn't.

"I established myself in this business, consulting with healthcare professionals, by offering a lower price for my services," Melinda told us. "If I raise prices now, I'll lose my advantage. Have you ever had the head of a nursing team mad at you? It's no fun. Nurses are like wolverines when they turn on you. I have to face facts here. Prices are the main reason these people are working with me."

Melinda had painted herself into an unnecessary psychological corner.

I explained to her the faulty logic in her approach.

"Melinda, you yourself have to shift the focus of the discussion from price to value," I told her. "Even if they ask about price, tell them your price and shift the conversation back to the value. Create value!"

"Well, I'm just worried," Melinda said. "Sometimes I have money issues and self-worth issues of my own."

"Leave those behind," I said. "Focus on the outcome of your work. Stand for it. Stand strong for the outcome. Your consulting gets good results, right?"

"Yes it does," she agreed.

"Then stay focused on that value. You are not a commodity. They can only get your unique consulting from you. They can't get it anywhere else. You, however, can get money and clients anywhere. You don't need them, they need you. They will pay you what you think you are worth. And the more they pay you, the more they will value your work."

Melinda finally decided to accept our advice and the small business truth that raising your prices is a good thing to do. She just held her nose, and spoke the new fees to anyone interested in her services. She also explained to existing customers that her original fees were purely introductory. If they wanted to do future work they would have to pay the fees that were standard, and if they didn't care to do that she was okay with that. She understood, and it didn't bother her because there were plenty of clients waiting to use her.

Melinda was shocked by the results of her fee increase. Some existing customers complained, and two even left her (one came back later). But with every new client she acquired she was surprised to see that her increased prices didn't seem to matter to them at all. They were just as eager to receive her services as the earlier clients were. In fact, once they paid the higher fees, they were more likely to keep their appointments and to do their homework! Their commitment to the outcome of the consulting was deeper, so the consulting had taken on more power from *the raising of the prices alone.* Soon she was learning to sell value rather than price, and so value was what they bought.

"I found that the more I charged, the more they valued my time," Melinda said. "I don't know why I had just assumed that lower prices would be good for them and appealing to them. Maybe it was because price was always the first thing they asked about, so I just assumed it was the most important thing on their mind."

I learned this lesson early in his seminar career. I used to offer an "introductory pilot seminar" to Fortune 500 companies interested in his training.

I had noticed that at the free introductory seminar, people would wander in late, people would take cell calls during my talk, and the attendance was low. One day, the president of a major bank asked for one of my introductory seminars so its managers could preview my work. I said "sure," and quoted him a very large price. The bank president stopped and stared at me.

"You're going to charge me that much just to preview your program?" he asked.

"Yes I am," I said.

"How do you justify that?" he asked.

"I want your people to value the time they give me and the time I give them," I explained. "My seminars carry the power to change lives, shift thinking forever, right on the spot. But they won't do that if there's no commitment from you or your people. Commitment is a two-way street. When you are committed you listen differently. I need your people listening as if their lives hung in the balance. And you will also see that after the seminar my time was worth that money to you. I am not a freebie. I cannot move your people from their fixed victim positions if I'm a freebie, a human handout."

The bank president wrote me a check that very day.

What happened in that room that day was much different than what used to happen in my free intro seminars. People showed up early, got good seats, and took notes. The level of consciousness was different. Money commits people.

The Basic Math Is Very Simple

The biggest damage unnecessarily low prices can do to your business is obvious. It's simple math. Low prices mean you simply make less money on each transaction. You have less to live on, less to spend on effective marketing, and less to pay to good employees. You also have less to save for a rainy day, less strength in your business, and less pride in your work.

And there's yet another damaging impact to your business that low prices cause. (Are you starting to be convinced here?) It's subtler, but just as toxic: Low prices attract more questionable customers. The customers you attract who are just shopping price are not the kinds of customers you want in the long run, anyway!

To build a business that serves you, instead of a business that you are constantly serving, you want to keep improving the quality of your customers. You want loyal, long-term customers. You want people who can afford your services over and over again. You want people who refer others like them. Low prices don't attract that kind of repeat customer.

Small business truth: Low prices attract disloyal, unfaithful *people*. People you can't build a business on.

When we bring people into our seminars we often hear them say, "My customers are cheap and all they care about is price!" Well, how did you produce that situation? It takes a while to get these people to see that *they themselves* have actually created that situation by believing the lie that lower prices boost business.

Your Customers Get What They Pay For

The two companies with the largest repeat car purchases in the United States are Cadillac and Lexus. And they also happen to be two of the most expensive cars on the market. The most expensive cars have the most repeat purchases? Wouldn't you think that repeat purchases would occur wherever people were getting the "best deal" on a car?

> **Small business truth:** *The more people pay for something, the more they value it.*

With Cadillac and Lexus owners, the larger price they pay makes them more eager to love and care for their vehicles. They then do all the things necessary to really get their money's worth out of their buying experience. They take better care of their cars, and so the cars serve them longer and better, and retain more value. It's a never-ending positive cycle! The more people pay, the better they appreciate what they have. When your customers pay you top price, *they will help you make sure it has been a valuable purchase.* Keep that in mind: They will help you justify the price.

Yes, your customers will do that for you! The more you charge them, the more their behavior changes for the better. Soon, they'll be referring others, because they want to feel good about their decision to commit a real investment into your services. Now they have a stake in making this buying experience valuable, and they will help you make your value a reality.

Sam experienced a similar example of this phenomenon.

"We had just bought a new building for our business," he recalled. "We had to get about $5,000 worth of signage for it. We sent out the quotes and began looking at options and prices. In the end, we didn't just pick the cheapest sign company to do the job, because we eventually had more respect for the gentleman whose prices were more expensive. He even explained why his signs were more expensive. And that helped close the sale! We appreciated the pride he had in his business. We didn't want to save a couple of hundred dollars going with the cheapest company. If they don't have much respect for themselves, we didn't think they were going to have as much respect for the work they would do."

You think your low price is showing respect for your customer. It's not. It's showing a *lack* of respect for your customer and for yourself. If you *appreciate yourself enough* to raise your prices and say, "I'm worth it," then people will know you are worth it. People will value you to the degree that you value yourself. Remember that every prospective customer of yours believes deep down that "you get what you pay for." He or she has probably even said that phrase out loud numerous times in his or her life. Have you allowed the customer to apply his or her insight to your business?

Get on the Magic Carpet of Higher Price

The next time you get an envelope full of coupons (the kind you always get in the mail) take a look at them. You might have even decided once to use a discount coupon to clean your carpet—three rooms for $50! But did you respect that cleaner when they came? Or did you have to hire a security firm to watch them? At the very least you probably thought, "Here are some cheap people desperate for the business."

We know a carpet cleaner who charges more than any carpet cleaner in southern California. He cleans the homes of celebrities and CEOs. He says, "If your house isn't worth a half million dollars or more, don't call me, because I'm too expensive for you. If you're in a rental place, or if your house isn't a very expensive house, you won't want to pay what I charge. You won't be able to afford it."

And people flock to him! He's the person every-one wants. People love knowing that they have risen to the level of being able to use him. And for a carpet cleaner—really!

People would gladly pay *you* more if you gave them a reason. The best reason of all is the belief you have in yourself. People will pay more for that than anything else.

We Only Fear What We Don't Understand

Understand your fear of raising prices. Don't run away from it. You need to know *going in* as you start thinking about money and prices that there's going to be fear in there. Don't let the fear make decisions for you. Acknowl-edge the fear, set it aside, and then make a very creative, nonemotional decision regarding your prices.

Then, when you talk to your customers, in person and in advertising, talk value. Tell stories about other happy customers and what they have experienced. Do not talk price unless you have to. Talk value. Be enthu-siastic. Enthusiasm is contagious. Your customer wants you to believe in yourself. Drop all the false modesty and sing and soar and come alive when you have the opportunity to talk about what your business does. Be an excited, live infomercial. Because customers love that! They want to buy from someone who is *proud* and *happy* about what they do.

And when it comes time to talk price, be even prouder. Be a sunbeam when you say your price. You love your price. It's bigger and more beautiful than the competitor's price because of how much benefit the customer receives from you. You love that price. You say it easily, the way a proud parent talks about a little child. The way a happy grandparent brags about a grandchild. You are in love with what your business does for people.

When you raise your prices, you'll soon have more money, and therefore you have something—the extra cash—that you can use to create even more customers, and even better customers. You'll be able to market, advertise, and promote in ways you couldn't afford to before.

What Does a Cup of Coffee Cost?

Starbucks is currently a very visible refutation of the low-price lie. They are a lesson to the world. Go on a business field trip to a Starbucks. Take your employess. Show them how it works. The next time you are inside Starbucks, really take in the whole experience and atmosphere and learn from it. Because you can do a version of Starbucks yourself.

Perhaps more than any company, Starbucks has shown that you can raise prices on a very basic product (coffee, cookies, and milk!) and if you do it creatively, people will not only pay more, they will provide you with a loyal, almost cultlike, following of your business.

Unlike the greasy little coffee shop on the corner, Starbucks is not projecting poverty or scarcity. When you walk into Starbucks you're experiencing a classy, tasteful, high-value environment. There's beauty in the design and atmosphere. Beauty! (Add beauty to your business when you get back home from Starbucks. Add beauty to your price, too.)

You go to Starbucks for the whole experience. (The buying experience! Think in terms of enhancing and improving the buying *experience*!) You notice that there are people who love to go there just to hang out in Starbucks. They keep buying expensive items just to hang out.

Even though your rational mind says, "This is just coffee with milk in it. I could have made my own and brought it to the park bench instead of coming to Starbucks," you still find yourself plopping down a $10 bill and getting very little change back for your drink. Not to mention waiting in line to do it! And we do this because our emotional self says, "Yes, I like doing this. It makes me feel good to come in here."

Sell to your customer's emotional side. All purchases are emotional, anyway, although your customer may put up a good show of talking price with you. Don't be misled by his desire to look tough-minded on price in front of his spouse. Don't be misled into thinking people buy based on price.

And please don't have *this* be your slogan: "The best quality, the best service, the best prices!" That slogan will drag your business down into the pits. We work with hundreds of businesses, and we have *never* seen that slogan serve anyone.

Don't Learn From Big Business

It could be that small business owners get tangled up in this low-price lie because they watch the behavior of corporate giants and think they must be worth emulating. They watch companies such as Wal-Mart and The Home Depot go to war on price and think, "That must be what business and marketing is all about."

But small business is different. It's more creative. Your opportunities to succeed are greater.

The truth is, you can take *very few principles* away from observing the corporate giants, because your advantages in your small business are the opposite of theirs. They have massive volume, distribution, and leveraging advantages you don't, so don't be misled by their price war behavior. It doesn't apply to you. Thank goodness!

For example, you'll want to resist shoring up the low-price lie by adding the related falsehood that you will "Make It Up In Volume." A lot of people fall for this fallacy, thinking, "Here's my pricing strategy. I'm going to make my prices low and I'm going to make it up in volume." Like the guy who buys a whole chain of money change-making machines. And someone says, "Well, wait a minute, how will you make a profit? People put in a dollar and you give them four quarters. How can you possibly make any money on that?" And he says, "Well I'm going to make it up in volume."

We were looking in the paper a couple of days ago and saw a person advertising his furnace-cleaning business. He had a small ad that said absolutely nothing compelling about why anyone should give him a call. It was just, "EJS Furnace Cleaning, We Clean Furnaces and Ducts, and here's our phone number."

What is the reader of the ad going to think? What is going to attract him or her? Is this a *new* thing, that someone can clean my furnace?

But what if this cleaner had a properly constructed ad that was a half page in size and actually had very compelling things that called out to the reader? You may think the owner couldn't afford a larger ad, but with higher prices he could have!

Are You Bartering in a Flea Market?

When we ask small business people in a seminar, "Who here thinks they can raise their prices between 15 and 20 percent right now and have absolutely no problem making more money next year, and not lose customers, and not worry about that? Who here can do that without worry?" You see very few hands go up, if any. They are scared.

Their fear comes from that whole small business self-esteem factor that says, "I'm not worth it. I'd feel guilty because my customers already trust me for this price and I'm betraying them by charging them more."

Trust and betrayal? That sounds like daytime soap opera television. This is not a soap opera about trust and betrayal, this is a business. A business is no more than fun and games with numbers! There's no value in taking the game of pricing this seriously, talking about "trust" and "betrayal" and all the frightening concepts that money and scarcity might be bringing forward. A price is just a number. No need to make it creepy.

Get yourself back into that state of mind you were in when you first started your business. That fun-and-games state of mind when you were up all night with the positive possibilities. Never lose that *game element* that buoys every business's energy and creativity.

It's odd, because one evening, after a grim day at work, you may go home and look for a way to relax and have fun. Soon you find yourself playing a strategic board game against friends and relatives and really feeling light-hearted and great about it. Your mental energy and creativity are carefree and inventive, even though you had thought you were exhausted. You were "tired," but now you're *not* because you've got a game going! Let the games begin! You're in a higher creative state because you know it doesn't matter if you lose or win, it's just flat-out fun playing the game. So you apply all kinds of fresh, wacky, and bold strategies in your board game, and you find that your thinking can be really effective.

But then the next day you go back to your business, and the overriding feelings are all back. What a hassle! What a grind. No, it's worse than a grind. It's frightening: *I mean, this could all go away, I could lose everything!* And there's nothing resembling the game element of the night before, there's just serious business going on.

Knock it off! Stop it with the heavy stuff!

The heavy, end-of-the-world thinking has to be changed. For you to succeed, that fear problem of yours has to be solved once and for all. You must stop being so serious about everything. It's bringing everyone down. You. Your family. Your customers. Everyone. Instead of playing into your own fear, why not play the great game of business every day? Why not treat your challenges as you would a strategic board game? Ask yourself carefree questions such as, "What could I do in my business to raise my prices by 20 percent and be confident I could keep all my customers and get many more new customers?"

Now It Is Time to Sell Your House

It may help you see the truth in this if you think of your business as a house. Let's say you bought an average kind of house and you bought it in order to sell it someday down the line. What could you do to that house to make it worth more money in the eyes of the buyer? You would probably get very creative about increasing its value, wouldn't you? You would go to the library, or go on the Internet, where the realtors tell you the things to do to your house to increase the perceived value of it the most for the next sale. You'd watch the popular TV home makeover shows. You would have real fun raising the price by raising the value. Soon you might go into the kitchens and bathrooms and lightly renovate those rooms. Then you would plant a few flower beds. In the end, you know you could get much more for the house than you paid for it if you set your mind to it. You would see it as a game, because it's all a game.

But what about your business? Why aren't you willing to do the same thing? The same principle applies! Exactly the same.

It's free enterprise. It's called free enterprise, because it's best done free and easy. It's not called "serious, frightening, heavy enterprise." It's called "free enterprise." With creative pricing, you can free yourself and free your enterprise.

An episode of Donald Trump's *The Apprentice* aired a while back when we were collecting our thoughts about what we would put in this book for you. As you may know, *The Apprentice* is a reality show that pits two teams against each other each week to see which team solves a new business problem more efficiently. The task on this week's show was to sell a brand new line of M&M candy bars on the streets of New York. The team that made the most money within a given time period would win.

One team (two men and a woman) went out into the streets offering a "nice low price" for the big tasty bars, selling them for two dollars each. And after a discouraging beginning, the team soon began to panic and lower their prices even further to a dollar a bar. (They had bought in to the *lie* that lower prices boost business.)

The other team (two women) came out of the chute with a happy confident attitude, dressing themselves up as the attractive, fun-loving Candy Bar Twins (free enterprise), and selling the same candy bars for five dollars each! They made the buying experience so much fun, and they were so confident in their product and price, that they sold a ton of candy bars at five dollars while the other team *couldn't sell them* for two dollars each.

The exact same market, the exact same product—just a different mindset.

We see this example over and over. Raise the value of the buying experience and raise your prices and you will not lose customers, you will gain them.

Lie #

6

You Have to Be Tightfisted

Some of the biggest charitable givers in history were also some of the most successful entrepreneurs.

They didn't give money because they made so much of it. They gave because they were givers. They started giving through their business. The image of the miserly rude Scrooge-type boss just isn't the truth. It's a creation of the media.

No one likes hanging out with friends so cheap that when you go out to a restaurant they pull out a calculator and calculate exactly how much they owe and exactly how much the tip should be. People don't want to deal with that kind of business either.

A major mistake that small business managers make begins with a good impulse: the impulse to be responsible with money and the positive desire to control costs and hold yourself accountable.

But as good as that desire is, it soon morphs into a twisted falsehood. It changes from frugal to tightfisted. It goes from smart to stupid.

It takes on the deep fear and anxiety that come with a sense of scarcity and mistrust. Then we see frugality's miserly dark side. That's when it becomes a negative mentality, a close-handed, tightfisted mentality that blocks so many wonderful avenues for creativity and growth.

The best way to insure that this does not happen to you is to adopt the operating principle we call *Open Hand*. It will serve you all your days. It will keep your business growing.

Let's get a clear picture of the principle by using a metaphor that can lead you to a philosophy that attracts customers at a dizzying rate. Imagine you are standing in a sandbox and you are reaching down to scoop up a handful of sand. You want as much sand as you can get, so you keep your hand as open as you can because an open hand holds the most sand.

But look at what happens the minute you start to worry. The minute you worry that you will lose your sand, or that someone may knock it from your hand, you clench your hand and squeeze it tight. Notice what that does to the volume of sand. You have less and less sand. The more you close your hand, the less you have. The tighter you squeeze, the less you have. That's the problem with being tightfisted.

Now think of that sand as your money. The money your business has to work with. The more tightfisted you are, the less money you have. So the object will be to learn the reverse approach—the approach known as *Open Hand*. Because good things happen when you open your hand and let the sand flow, both in and out of your business. The more open-flow you maintain, the more dynamic your business can be. Trapped is bad. Flowing is good.

It Works Wherever You See It

The great department store giant Nordstrom built their entire legendary business by using *Open Hand* while all their competitors were tightfisted. Nordstrom applied *Open Hand* to their merchandise return policy as just one example of their trust and generosity toward their customers. If you wanted to return something to Nordstrom, they were happy to do it, no questions asked. Did you wear it? *That's okay.* Can you not find your receipt? *Doesn't matter. We trust you. Just bring it back.*

Their competitors, meanwhile, were being tightfisted. They demanded receipts, they made you jump through hoops, they did not trust you at all. They treated you as a potential criminal. Something to return? Put your hands up! We are suspicious of you!

Soon the word spread throughout the land that Nordstrom was different. A different kind of store. More classy. More generous. More trusting and accommodating. In short, a purely pleasurable buying experience.

Because of their Open Hand policy, and the number of urban legends it was creating (stories of Nordstrom's "irrational" generosity towards customers spread like wildfire), Nordstrom didn't have to spend as much on advertising as their competitors. Their customers were doing the bulk of the advertising for them! The stories they told! The stories went over backyard fences, spread through neighborhoods and family gatherings. One woman returned an item Nordstrom didn't even sell and received a full refund! Amazing!

One of the reasons so many businesses lapse into the tightfisted mentality is that they see each customer in isolation, as a one-time singular purchase. They then try to milk that experience for all the money it's worth. The business owners don't realize that this customer is actually bigger than that. They don't see that this customer is a potential lifelong repeat purchaser, *if treated right*, and a network of referrals, *if treated right*.

Businesses don't see that being stingy with a customer on a refund policy or not responding to a complaint shuts off future windfall profits in the name of milking the pennies out of this one, isolated deal.

Customers do not exist in isolation. They are part of networks. They are attached to webs. Pinch one customer and the whole web is hurt. Treat one person badly, and his or her whole network of contacts and relatives hears about it.

We all know the experience of dreading what the mechanic will say about fixing our car but then hearing him say, "We fixed it right away and there won't be any charge for that. We value your business here and appreciate all the opportunities you have given us to serve you, and for something small like this we aren't going to charge you."

A lot of business people would call that folly. They would say that you have to charge whenever and wherever you can; otherwise you are being financially irresponsible. After all, it all adds up. Even small fees for work add up at the end of the day. You have to tighten that fist.

But Open Hand works better. It creates a more generous flow into your business. Because the next time your car breaks down, you have no doubt where you are taking it. And the next time a coupon arrives at your home announcing a new mechanic in town, you don't even look at it. The next time your brother-in-law calls you asking where you get your car done, you don't hesitate to urge him to go to your mechanic and say, "Tell him who you are, they know me there, they'll take good care of you."

All of this for 30 dollars! He waived a 30-dollar fee for all of this. The Open Hand mechanic creates new customers all day long with Open Hand. He also nails down his customer base so that he doesn't have defectors. A family that started with him three years ago now has three cars to service, not just one. Open Hand can triple his business without a penny spent on advertising.

Most people lose half their sand by squeezing their hand.

Recently we asked a struggling restaurant owner named Ralph if he might consider giving his customers a gift certificate for a complimentary dessert and coffee the next time they came in. Ralph was horrified at the idea.

"Let me explain my business to you," said Ralph. "If I have a $50 bill at the end of the evening, when you factor all my labor, food, rent costs, and so on, into it I am not making all that much profit on the $50! It's tight! To give away dessert and coffee would be to cut into that profit even further, and it just doesn't make good business sense to do it."

Ralph's first tightfisted mistake was to see the customer as a mere $50 dining bill. He saw the customer in the narrow isolation of a single buying experience, whereas Open Hand looks at the customer from two different viewpoints: (1) He or she is a lifelong source of repeat business and (2) he or she will deliver us multiple referrals. From those two standpoints, coffee and dessert are a very tiny price to pay to encourage that customer to return and refer.

Without a basic Open Handed philosophy, you will miss opportunities throughout the day to add value to your customer's buying experience. Every time you open your hand to add value, you increase your referrals and repeat business. You get the stories going.

Your business will really take off once the stories about you start getting told. Those stories won't happen if you just satisfy your customer. Satisfied customers don't talk. They expect to be satisfied.

Customer relations in North America has taken a turn for the better, but it's still down around 10 percent of what it really could be. You can blow past your competition if you really tune into this potential for your business.

In the 1940s and 1950s the operative slogan for customer relations was "the customer is always right." It's not too hard to see why that slogan didn't last long. It's simply not true. The customer is not always right. The customer is often a jerk—but you don't want to have that be your slogan either. So businesses moved up to the more functional mission of *customer satisfaction*. However, in the highly competitive global marketplace, the idea of customer satisfaction began to run down. Somehow there was something wrong with it and soon it became clear—satisfaction is simply not enough. Satisfied customers don't talk—they are silent. They're flatliners. Why? Because people today *expect* to be satisfied. If they are satisfied, they are quiet. It's when they're not satisfied that they talk. Today's customers will deliver the most precious advertising of all—word of mouth—only if we go beyond satisfaction. We must truly delight the customer so that the customer will talk.

We had been giving seminars in customer delight for a long time when a homebuilder by the name of Gary Gietz took one of our courses and decided it wasn't exciting enough for him. He absorbed everything taught, then he took it to a whole new dimension by insisting that his company, Gary Gietz, Master Builders, shoot for *customer astonishment*. By holding his company to that standard— "We will astonish each and every customer with what we do"—he has rapidly become one of the premier luxury home builders in the world. But he attained something else even more valuable. By teaching his people and even his vendors and customers how to astonish other people, he created a game that people loved playing. He transformed the thinking of everyone who came in contact with him. He got people in touch with their latent inner creativity. Astonishment became a way of life.

Open Hand isn't just about customers. It's about anyone in your business world that you have a relationship with that's worth something to you. If you look at how to astonish the people around you, you're looking at the best of you and the best of them. We'd use a different word for it, but we can't. The results of this approach really are astonishing.

What the tightfisted business person does is try to attract people based on his own mistrust: the one-time hit! "Best prices! Best service! Best food!" Rather than interact in a friendly way with the entire lives of real people, they are always trying to appeal to those who have never come in, that amorphous inhuman mass of untrustworthy, price-shopping, predatory beings called the prospective customer base.

For Open Hand to become a part of a business's culture and way of being, we must constantly coach ourselves and our people about our customers' long-term value, instead of their one-time cash flow hit.

You Can Have a Big, Fat Greek Wedding

A Greek restaurant nearby has seen our own business grow because we bring our own employees in to the restaurant each year to celebrate that year's accomplishments. So a few years back the restaurant owner saw us with just a few people at our table, and a year later more people, and now he has to mark off almost a third of the restaurant to accommodate us. So, naturally, he became curious about our success and what made it happen. Soon he was even asking for ideas, so we gave him one. No charge.

This was during the time when the movie *My Big Fat Greek Wedding* was so popular, so we gave him what we thought was a marvelous promotional idea for his Greek restaurant. The movie had just come out on DVD, so we recommended that he find a way to purchase a large number of the DVDs and run a promotion wherein he would say (in his ads or in a banner in the window or on a neighborhood flyer): "Free copy of *My Big Fat Greek Wedding* for any dinner party of four!"

The idea was brilliant! Not only are you giving away something many people wanted, but you are forever linking the gift to your business. The Greek connection would forever remain in the customers' minds, and the loving and humorous portrayal of Greek Americans in the movie would forever be associated with your own business.

The idea was rejected. The restaurant owner's rationale for the rejection was this: "I don't want to pay $20 for that DVD and then just give it away! There goes all the profit on that meal. I'm not an idiot!"

Oh, but you *are*, sir. The reason is that all the money he spent on advertising, and all those nights where his restaurant was nearly empty he was still paying employees to stand around and do nothing but wipe tables over and over. And these realities cost him a *lot* more than the gift of the DVD would have cost.

And so you see why that restaurant owner may *never* know how to utilize Open Hand. His vision of his business is contracted down to the tightfisted view of the one-time hit.

Tragically, that same business owner will pump countless $20 bills into his advertising budget trying to attract new customers to the restaurant. Customers who may or may not ever come in. But spend $20 on someone already in the restaurant? Can't see the value.

Sam said to the owner, "Okay, do as you wish, but we grew our business that way, and you asked."

"Okay, okay," the Greek replied. "How about this? How about we give the DVD to first-time customers only? That way I can at least rationalize that it's going to new customers."

He still didn't get it. His return customers are even more valuable to him than any new customer would be, because his return customers are the ones who bring people in. Over and over. So he would be better off having a night where his longtime customers were feted with a free dinner of appreciation than he would trying to make sure all his expenditures went toward new business.

The tight fist does damage to a business. It punches out all the warmth and attractive generosity of a family feeling. The Open Hand caresses a business and causes it to grow.

Don't You Just Hate to Give Refunds?

Let's get back to refunds. Most tightfisted businesses hate to give full refunds. They give a refund minus certain elements, to milk that one-time hit. Whereas giving a full refund and being nice about it and happy to do it increases positive word of mouth and changes that unhappy customer back into a warm future prospect again.

By being stingy on refunds, the tightfisted small business owners are missing a major insight into how the entire universe is set up. Humanity is a network of interconnected beings. People don't live in isolation. Yet the tight fist treats each customer as if he lives in a closed-off cave of isolation. As if he won't talk! As if he can't refer! As if he'll just walk away and never communicate with anybody!

But when I commit to being an Open Hand owner I will think differently and teach all my people to behave differently. I will see that everybody is connected to everybody else. Any one person on this planet is just a phone conversation or an e-mail away from any other person on this planet. Once I truly see that, I start treating every one of my customers differently.

The whole belief that people will take advantage of me and that I might lose my shirt comes from an inner programming of scarcity and fear. It is quite often a projection of my own business's feeling of scarcity on the customer. Sometimes it can be a projection of my own personal mistrust and fear on the customer. And unless I am willing to correct this projection, it will eventually be fatal to my business.

Open Hand benefits go even further than we think. Open Hand can be more than a good business strategy, it can be a way of living. Most people think that they're just in their business to make a profit, not realizing that the true potential of their business is to grow into much more than that. It can grow into a way of life. And this is not just some ideal scene. It's really almost a must!

Because you don't want to build a business that you're afraid of. You don't want to wake up every day afraid of something bad happening. You don't want a daily vision of losing everything. No one does. No one says, "I started this business so that I could know what it felt like to be afraid of losing everything." No one starts a business for that.

Instead, you can have a whole new abundant way of living that you get from your business. A giving, flowing way of dealing with people, dealing with customers, dealing with employees and vendors. You can create a way of life while you're creating your business. Why must they be separate? Your customers will pick up on that way of life, too. They will see how you are living, and it will be something they are drawn to. If it's generous and positive, they will tell stories about you.

5 New Ideas You Should *Not* Follow

Recently a local newspaper ran a brief business advice article called "Five Tips on Starting a Business." It was a wonderful example of how bad advice and common sense go hand in hand, and why people fail at business. They fail because they read articles like these and take them to heart.

These kinds of articles soon become part of the common "sense" being spread around about small business, and it's not long before you have nine lies to fix before you go under.

The first tip this article recommended was that you "keep costs and spending down. Businesses fail because they have too much overhead."

Not true! Businesses fail because "keeping costs down" is given priority over growing your business, attracting the right kind of customer, and allowing the principle of Open Hand to full you up with prosperity. This "tip" is negative and reactive, rather than positive and proactive, and it is based on a psychology of fear and scarcity. You can't *save your way* to success in business.

Tip number two recommended that you "take the time to create a business plan. That means doing a marketing study, looking at the competition, costs, and prices." Again, that's reactive rather than creative. Do you think Starbucks looked at the price of coffee at every Denny's and every little corner coffee shop before deciding on its pricing? No. They created a plan based not on the market or the competition, but on their ideal good customer. The old, worn-out, failed wisdom that shows up in this "tip" allows the market and competition to dictate your vision, which is backwards! Let the market and the competition respond to you!

Tip number three said that "theory is valuable, but you have to adapt it." Well, no. If the theory is valuable, as is our theory that "advertorials," or information-rich, benefit-rich, problem-solving large ads draw more good customers than "getting the word out" does, then you just have to use it. What's important here is that you find a theory of business success that is proven to work, and then you use it as directed. You don't have to "adapt" it.

Tip number four claimed owners should "Persevere and talk to other business owners." This can be a very bad idea on both fronts. First of all if you persevere in the wrong direction it's worse for you than changing directions. For example, persevere in bad pricing that's too low, and you'll cause yourself real problems. Persevere in advertising that doesn't connect, and you lose more money than if you pull the ad campaign as soon as it fails to produce what you want it to.

And as for "talk to other business owners," we wonder why? If four out of five business owners fail soon after they are started, why talk to them? What can they tell you? You have an 80 percent chance of getting very bad advice. In fact, what you will hear from failing business owners are the nine lies we are discussing!

The newspaper article then went on to say, "You'll soon learn that it takes more years than you planned to get your business off the ground." Not if you know what you're doing! Our clients succeed right away! Again, this widespread falsehood that is being spread as the truth. If your business is good, and you are creative about developing a large base of happy customers, your business will succeed right away! How can it not?

And here's their last tip the newspaper article offered: "*Keep believing.*"

In what?

Business success is not a matter of blind faith. You can actually find out *consciously* how to succeed. It's not a matter of fervent hoping. It's not a matter of believing. It's not blindly trusting that things will break your way.

Belief is not what you need. You need a plan. You even have to be willing to drop any belief you hold at any time on a dime if that belief isn't serving your business. Get the facts on what works. Verify them with successful businesspeople and consultants. Then move forward. What part does belief play in that?

Your success will not come from belief, it will come from certainty. As long as you live in the nebulous wonderland of hopes and dreams and beliefs then you lose your grip on what can be real assurance of success. Be certain. Know that you can *know* how to succeed.

Read up on Starbucks and Nordstrom and you'll get your certainty. The tightfisted owner drives customers away. The generous Open Hand draws customers in. You don't have to believe in it to know that it works. You don't have to believe in gravity to jump out of a burning building. You just have to use it.

You don't have to believe in Open Hand to benefit from it. You just have to use it.

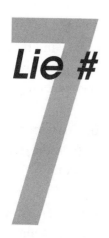

Lie

Customers Are Hard to Figure Out

Customers are mysterious! You never know where they're going to come from or what they're going to do next! They're like aliens from another planet. No wonder business is so hard and stressful.

Actually none of the above is true.

Customers are something you can learn about and understand. And where your business success is concerned, knowledge is power. Customers' buying behavior is not hard to figure out or anticipate. If you apply enough brain power and study, you'll know exactly what to do to make your business fill up with happy, quality customers.

Not just any customers, but good ones. Good customers who repeat their business and refer other people to you.

Not the one-hit wonders who shop for price or premium and then disappear into the night never to be seen again.

But it starts with you. You must be curious and thorough and make a comprehensive science out of studying your customer. From the minute he or she walks in the door!

"Hello, is this your first time visiting us?" is your first question to each new customer. Because it opens the door to so much knowledge, and knowledge is power.

If the answer is "yes," and this is his or her first time, you can proceed to give a tour or a talk and you can ascertain where the customer came from and what drew him or her to the store.

If the answer is "no," you can thank him or her for coming back in and talk about the customer's previous experience and buying preferences.

The more you know (and record as data) about your customer, the more prosperous your business will become.

Successful coaches in sports have long repeated the philosophy that the will to win is not the most important thing. What is most important is the will *to prepare* to win.

Knowing your customer is preparing to win.

And the minute you begin telling yourself the fib that they are hard to figure out is the minute you stop really building your business.

For you to really succeed in business, this relationship must be like a love affair. So, let's begin with how the two of you met.

Knowing how your customer found you is gold. Gold! Because as you track it, you can keep shaping where your marketing and promotion money goes, directing it toward what actually attracts people instead of letting it continue to leak out toward what doesn't. If most of your people are coming in from Yellow Pages, then it's time to redirect that radio money into the Yellow Pages. If people are coming in from referrals, it's time to enhance your referral program. Knowledge is power.

Most businesses have gold right under their noses that they fail to mine. Instead, they become random businesses reaching out in a random way to new customers, similar to those horrifying Hieronymous Bosch paintings of people reaching out from hell to be rescued. Those are people who do not know their customers!

Many businesspeople we coach have no clue. Not in the beginning. The owners have no clue as to how many customers they have, what customers' buying preferences have been, where the customers are from, what brought them in, or who they have referred! No clue!

The business owners often don't have a current mailing list to mine and cultivate because they don't have a mailing list at all. Therefore they are not consistent with their follow-ups, not realizing that follow-up communication is the best and most cost-efficient communication you can make for increased sales! It also keeps customers from defecting, and it inspires more referrals.

Dr. Chris Glawe is a veterinarian we know whose practice is thriving because of his follow-up. He has waiting lists of people who want to get in to see him because of his reputation. People say he is the best. People say he really, truly cares about their pets and regards their pets in the same way that a pediatrician regards your child. And what he does to convey this, is *he follows up.* He calls back a week after the visit to see how Spot is feeling this week. He may even call back again in another week!

But how does he do it? How does he have the time?

Dr. Glawe's call-back touch is so kind and caring that it locks his clients in to a lifetime of devoted loyal patronage at the highest fees in town. Across the street, Dr. Multitasker wrings his hands over how hard it is to get his business going and do all there is to do in a day. He thinks about how clients are so hard to figure out. Does he run a bigger ad in the Yellow Pages? Does he put up a billboard? How is he to know? It's all so hard to figure. People! Dumber than animals, most of them. Where will they take their business? Who knows? Go figure.

Your Greatest Asset as a Business Owner

The biggest asset you possess as a business owner is your mental energy. Most people would say that your greatest asset was your core competency, or your time, or your money, but none of that is true.

Your greatest asset is your mental energy. Where are you going to direct that? That's what will determine your failure or success.

If you put your mental energy into worry and doubt and fighting fires all day, then you will get more and more fires. If, on the other hand, you put your mental energy, your most precious asset, into understanding your customer, then you will get more and more customers.

Wherever you place your attention in your business, that area will grow. It's the law of the harvest. Your mental energy can be likened to sunshine: Wherever you shine it, things will grow. The businesses that know the most about their customers will grow their customer base the fastest.

During the dot-com craze in American business most businesses failed spectacularly because all their focus was on the innovative technology of the business itself, and none of the focus was on the customer. Amazon.com was the biggest exception. Amazon made their whole business revolve around customer information. Today we get e-mails from Amazon telling us our favorite author has just released a new book, or a message that they just found an out-of-print book we had been looking for a year ago, and would we like them to hold it for us? Amazon knows us the way an old friend does.

Contrast that to a local bookstore chain that, even though you are visiting them for the tenth time this year, treats you as cattle, shuttling you through the customer line (there are ropes! No whips yet, but ropes!) as if you are an irritating, anonymous animal that has to be cleared out. They don't know who you are, whether you've ever come in before, what you like to read, or anything else. *They don't know and they don't care.* That's why they have to tantalize you with HUGE DISCOUNT PRICES SLASHED ON BESTSELLERS to get you to increase the total of your onetime purchase.

This is the very inhumanity—man's inhumanity to man—that characterizes businesses that have no knowledge of their customers. This is the inhumanity that causes most businesses to fail.

Consider the movie *You've Got Mail.* It's a perfect study in this concept. They should show it at the Harvard Business School. You might want to rent it on DVD if you haven't seen it because it illustrates a major mistake small businesses make. The mistake that leads them to lie to themselves about their customer. How the customer is an adversary! An enemy! A problem! So hard to figure out! Impossible to understand! Greedy! Impulsive!

In *You've Got Mail,* Tom Hanks is an executive for a large bookstore chain. Meg Ryan owns a little children's bookstore on the corner of the street, and across the street from Meg is where Tom's huge new behemoth chain store will open a new location; thereby driving little Meg out of business. Why will Meg be forced to shut down her charming little business? The sheer volume and force of the large chain will shut her down. Those prices! Oh my goodness, we can't compete with those discounts! They are not just going to reduce prices on their books, they are going to SLASH them! Big corporate greed machine wiping out the little people!

So what does Meg do?

If she were our client, she would rub her hands in happy anticipation of how well her little store was going to do in contrast to the heartless giant across the street. Because Meg had so many advantages. She had story hours where she would read to the children. She had superior product knowledge about children's books. And she had been in business for 30 years (dating back to her mother's ownership of the store). This would allow her to have a customer database that would allow her to perform communication magic compared to the chain store.

But is that how the movie played out? No. Of course not. The movie had Meg meltdown at how utterly unfair all of this was. Incredibly, the movie had Meg decide that there was only one avenue she could take to counter the competition: Protest! That's right, a real old-fashioned Vietnam-era antiwar type of protest. Berkeley in the 60s! Tom Hayden, Jane Fonda, Abbie Hoffmann, and Meg Ryan! Meg's employees were holding signs up, "UNFAIR! UNFAIR! UNFAIR!"

But despite all kinds of media coverage for her righteous, pitiful protest events, she had to quit and shut down. And the only thing that saved the movie was her falling in love with Tom Hanks, he having been her secret e-mail chat companion all along. A greedy corporate giant with a heart of gold. Who would have guessed?

This movie was a great illustration of where *not* to put your mental energy (your most precious business asset). Meg put her energy into her worries and fears. Most small business people do.

But what if Meg had put her energy here: "Hey, let's use this big chain invasion as a fresh inspiration to follow up with our customers. Let's put together a marketing plan to get our previous customers back into the store. All those people who bought books for their kids years ago may have grandchildren by now. How about a book-for-your-grandchild program? Bring us a picture of your grandchild for our wall, and we'll give you a free children's book!

Let's gather all the kids' and grandkids' birthdates. What about giving people memberships to the store, and putting them on automatic buying plans? Let's brainstorm all of this. How about insisting that we come up with four things this week to make the business more of a top-of-the-line, preferred customer, premium-priced business?"

That might not have made much of a movie, but it would have kept her in business.

The more you know about your customer, the faster your business can prosper and the greater your advantage will be over any competition that moves in.

Where Have All the Flowers Gone?

This weekend we went to visit the store of a florist in our area that we had purchased flowers from a few times. They did very nice arrangements. But we drove by and they were gone! The business was shut down. It didn't even say, "We've moved."

And we drove away thinking, "How in the world can a florist go out of business?"

And the answer had to be obvious: They didn't think about their customers. They didn't track them and catalogue them and keep notes and files on them.

> **Small business truth:** *Customer knowledge is power. The more of it you've got, the more powerful your business becomes.*

Picture this: You phone up the flower shop or drop by, and you say "Hello, I'd like to spend $50 on flowers." And their very next question to you would be, "Okay, great. What are the flowers for?"

Why do they ask that? Because knowledge is power.

And you say, "An anniversary." The next question they ask you would be, "Terrific. Which anniversary is it?"

"Oh, it's number nine."

"Oh, really? Let me mark that down. Congratulations."

So how hard is it for them to make a note and say "number nine" and then when they're completing the order say, "Oh, just for our records, we just have to make sure we have all this stuff on file." And they get your name and address. And next year, they know it's going to be number 10! They could even ask if you would like to be on their automatic reminder service. They could have their customer person sitting there with a list of customer names that says "anniversaries," phoning them one week before, saying, "Hey, Mr. Johnson, I noticed last year you used us for your anniversary. I just wanted to say congratulations and happy anniversary again, and let you know we have a special arrangement that we can set up for you. Additionally, we can even deliver it at no charge, so you don't have to take care of anything. Would you like us to do that for you?"

Or if you own a bookstore, and you keep track of your customers and the books they like, there are all kinds of communications you can do. If a customer liked a certain book or mystery writer such as Robert B. Parker, and you got a review of another mystery writer who was called "another Robert B. Parker," then you would send a note to everyone who's bought Robert B. Parker with a review and say, "Come in and try this guy out." If you had a little bookstore, they would never go anywhere else, once you got them in your system.

As we mentioned before, most large chain bookstores today don't know who you are and don't care who you are. They don't treat you well when you're in there. They herd you through lines, and one of those rent-a-teenagers yells, "Next!" real loud. "NEXT!" It's the most inhuman way of dealing with people. And then they keep grumbling that they're losing business to the Internet.

Sam was in San Diego recently and utilized his Hertz Gold membership (where they put your name up on the board and they have your car ready). While doing so, he noticed some people who later attended his seminar also using Hertz Gold. Though he knew they were not rolling in dough (yet), he could see that they too wanted to avoid the hassle often associated with renting a car. In fact, it's likely they've gone the cheap route in the past where they wait for what seems to be hours, and get treated as unwelcome strangers.

"It cost more money to use Hertz Gold," Sam observed. "But I step right in there because my name's on the board. Yes, that's Mr. Beckford to you! I hop in the car, and I feel good about that. They treat me like they know me and were expecting me."

Just the fact that you do these customer-friendly things that other businesses are unwilling to do will boost your business so many ways! Your employees will start to get into the act, collecting more and more information for you. You will reward them for it and encourage it, and it will make business more fun. It adds a dimension to the business that wasn't there before. And when the customer talks to you, you can speak about your customer commitment with such happy confidence. When the customer says, "You're expensive," you can quickly say, "True! But when you factor everything you get from us, you won't think so. Let me talk to you about the personal attention and tailoring you get." And it just rolls off your tongue; you don't have to defend your price. When you know more about the customer, you can feel better about that stronger price. You can feel better about your marketing. You can feel better about everything.

Converting Our Failure to Your Success

One painful advantage we have in delivering this material is our own personal histories of business failure. We both had businesses fail totally, and both see that this book would have saved us.

I ran an advertising agency many years ago, and I operated inside a number of these lies. The Lower Prices lie was the one that really did me in, although I bought some of the others as well, which hastened my downfall. We lasted four years and crashed in flames and bankruptcy. If I had someone such as Sam Beckford coaching me back then I would have done just fine.

In my earlier books, I wrote extensively about my personal reinvention, and even my recovery from addiction through 12-Step work. Back then, I used to see signs on the walls in the meeting rooms of 12-Step recovery centers that said "Your Best Thinking Got You Here."

Sam and I are tempted to say that same thing to the failing business owners we often encounter in our work. Because the business managers tell us all the reasons they are doing what they are doing, and in the course of the sessions we find that they have bought almost all of the nine lies we revealed in this book. Sometimes one person will tell us all of them! The conversation will go similar to this:

"Glad to have you people on board as my coaches," says Vern. "This has been a bad year for me."

"How so?" asks Sam.

"Well, I put myself in a bind from the start," Vern says. "We all know it takes money to make money, but I started this thing without much and had to borrow a lot along the way to make up for short times and now the debt is killing me. But how else do we pay for the advertising? I mean, you've got to get your name out there, right? Well, nobody makes a profit in a small business until year four, anyway, so I'm waiting for that to kick in, and in the meantime we're doing some massive discounting and price-cutting to stimulate business for the rest of this season. We're doing other things to help us out, like eliminating refunds and eliminating our repeat customer thank you mailings. Normally I never would have asked for help. It's a sign of weakness, right? But I heard good things about you guys, and a lot of circumstances this year, circumstances beyond our control, have hit us hard. A new competitor just opened, and the economy in our town took a dive and state regulations are tightening the noose on us. We've been victims of a lot of things we couldn't do anything about."

"Those new state regulations?" I ask.

"Yes, they are killing us!"

"Do they apply to your competitors, too?"

"Well, yes," answers Vern.

"Are you ready to start your business up?" asks Sam.

"What do you mean by that?" asks Vern.

"Your business is like a car that has never left the garage," says Sam. "It's time you started it up to see what it can do. But first we'll have to change a few things."

"Sure, of course," says Vern. "Where do you want to start?"

"You," I say. "Let's start with you. We're going to eliminate your entire belief system and replace it with something that runs. We're going to start you up."

Vern's thoughts and stories about why his business is hurting are enough to make a grown man cry. But they are typical of people caught upstream of business without a paddle. Four out of five new businesses fail, and they talk trash to each other. They spread the word on how *not* to succeed, and it's damaging to the psyche because it's all fear-based mythology.

To know how to succeed in business is inseparable from knowing your customer. You can't have one without the other.

We have created a little checklist for people such as Vern to study, memorize, and then get into their soul:

Focus on Your Ideal High-Value Customers and Ignore the Rest

$ You don't want every customer for your business. A lot of small business owners make a big mistake by thinking that they should try to get any customer they can.

$ Most small businesses are capacity businesses. That means you can only accommodate and service a maximum amount of business and customers.

$ Think of a hotel. If a hotel in busy season has 100 rooms and 90 of those rooms are filled by kids on spring break, it may have to turn away a lot of much better customers because it has reached capacity. A business traveler with an expense account who uses room service and will not steal items from the minibar is a much better customer for the hotel.

$ Don't waste time and money attracting customers that are bad for your business. Think of your best possible customers at your business now: the customers who never complain about your prices; the customers who think your service and quality is better than your competitors; the customers who pay their bills on time; the customers who were referred to you by other good customers or constantly refer business to you. Those are the types of customers you should focus on attracting more of.

$ Where did your best customers come from? The Yellow Pages? Then advertise heavily in the Yellow Pages!

$ Where did your worst, most problematic "cheapskate" customers come from? The discount coupon book you ran an ad in? Stop advertising in the coupon book and advertise more in the sources that produce higher-quality customers.

$ Poll your best customers you have right now, ask how they originally found your business. If you're doing a good job they'll be glad to tell you and help you grow your business.

For someone such as Vern, this checklist looks difficult. And we wouldn't give it to him unless we had also worked with him extensively on lies number one and number nine.

Remember that lie one says that all Vern has to do is know *how to* succeed. Not true. First Vern has to *want to* succeed. So we would work with Vern to tuneup his *want to* until it became a passion with him. If you want something badly enough, you'll have enough energy to do whatever it takes to get it! That's where we'd need Vern to be.

Then we'd have to jump to lie nine, the one Vern tells himself every day about being a victim of circumstance. Vern would need to shift from being a victim to being an owner. The good news is that anyone can make this shift. I describe how to make that shift in my book, *Reinventing Yourself*, and we would definitely give that book to Vern. (We will give the book to you, too, if you like. Just visit our Website at *www.smallbusinesstruth.com* and let us know you want it.)

Vern would ask Sam, "Any chance, after all is said and done, I could be a millionaire like you? With my small business?"

"Of course," Sam would say. "But to be successful, truly successful, you must understand all parts of the picture. Being successful is not just understanding how to make a profit from a small business, it's also a way of thinking and a way of being that you, the business owner, adopt. I believe that becoming a millionaire is not just about having a million dollar net worth, it is about thinking about yourself, about others, and about the world around you in a way that lets you attract success and maintain an upward spiral in your business and in your life."

"Is that why your customer knowledge list feels so strange to me?" Vern asks.

Yes, Vern. That's why. Because you have not made that transformation inside yourself that awakens the curiosity and compassion you need to succeed. One of the real signs that you love someone is how curious you are about them. How are they feeling? How are they doing? Where did they come from? What do they like? What do they prefer?

That kind of compassionate curiosity takes an internal shift away from fear. Fear is truly the enemy here. Lack of money is not the enemy. The competition is not the enemy. Fear is.

"The whole belief that people will just take advantage of me, and I'll lose my shirt, that comes from a scarcity mentality and fear," Sam explains. "And really, what our work is all about is not just about making money. I think it's about living your whole life in a certain way."

"Well, okay," says Vern. "But you say here that I should find out where my 'most problematic' customers come from. Can I afford to think that way? I need every customer I've got. Even the difficult ones. I can't start getting choosy at this stage, I'm in real trouble here."

And a lot of businesspeople make Vern's mistake. They fill their business with customers they don't want by trying to be fair and thinking, "Well, I guess we have to try and attract everyone, and anyone that wants to do business with us has to do business with us and we're obligated because, after all, they represent money."

And that's the heart of the problem right there. Customers are not money! They are people. And my business fortune shifts the minute I get this and apply it.

"I remember I was in Palm Springs during spring break a few years ago, and I saw a sign in this ice cream store that was pretty funny," said Sam. "It said, 'We reserve the right to refuse service to anyone, no matter how rich you are, how famous you are, or who your daddy is.' I liked that one. Obviously, in an area like Palm Springs, they're getting a lot of people that may be rich, famous, or have daddies that are, who knows! But if you're an owner, not a victim, you don't take everyone's business!"

Vern says, "I've always operated under the principle that says 'The Customer's Always Right.'"

"It's a lie!" exclaims Sam. "Customers will turn that against you. I mean, that's a huge lie, and that's something that small business people have to really work against, because the customer isn't always right. Sometimes they're very wrong and sometimes they're not just wrong, they're downright dangerous to you."

I chimed in, "There's another impact on this, too, Vern, that I think is important in turning away a customer. And that is the boost in morale if you have employees or partners or coworkers, and they witness that you have declined the business of a customer because that customer just does not treat people correctly, and you will not subject your employees to it. The boost in morale is tremendous to the whole group when they witness that."

"It is?" asks Vern.

"Yes, it is," agrees Sam. "Our rule is that if someone is going to be painful and abusive and not the right kind of person to deal with, we don't want them. And we give our people the ability and the judgment to say, 'This is the wrong type of customer for us.' And when we do that, when we've gotten rid of customers, we've gone as far as refunding everything. And this is just an interesting thing with the Open Hand concept. A lot of people, when it comes to refunds, they're just very tight. They say, 'No! That's my money! They paid for it and I'm going to get it, and that's not fair, they don't deserve that.'"

"How do you do it in your business?" asks Vern.

"We take the opposite approach," Sam explains. "If it's someone that's problematic, we basically are paying for our freedom. I'm happy to be able to say, 'Guess what, you've used $500 worth of services here, but this is not the place for you. We're not making you happy and it doesn't make sense for you to be in a place where you can't be happy, so here is your money back, and here are four other places you should go and try. I hope you can have a better experience there, because this is not the place for you.'"

"That would be hard for me," says Vern. "I mean, that $500 I'm giving them is my hard-earned money."

"Well, first of all, that whole hard-earned money thing— I hate that phrase," says Sam. "I hate the phrase hard-earned money because it implies that any money you get from any-where is hard or earned. And there's some money that's not hard or earned; there's some money that's very easily earned. But if you attach pain and sweat and frustration to every dollar you get, I just think, psychologically, when you go in and you have to make money for your business, it's going to be unnecessarily hard! Because sometimes the money you make in a small business is very easily earned money."

Vern had lost sight of the whole point of opening his own business. All the reasons he once listed for wanting to have his own business are now gone. He has turned his back on them now that he is inside his own business.

Sam wanted Vern to see that once you purge these lies from your system, a lot of your money is easily-earned, not hard-earned.

"After we had reached success in our own business, Vern, my wife and I used to take my in-laws to dinner," said Sam. "My in-laws have a very positive work ethic, and I'm not against hard work. I don't want to say that our coaching is like all those other Internet coaching scams where 'You can make a million dollars in your sleep, while doing absolutely no work, simply by taking one magic pill.' It's not like that at all. You do have to work hard, but the idea of years and years of struggle and backbreaking labor, and attaching that whole feeling to the money is not necessary. Anyway, my in-laws would say to me as I picked up the check for a very nice dinner, 'We don't want you to be spending all this money, because you're spending your hard-earned money taking us out to dinner.' And I always said, 'Well, actually I have two accounts and this money here is the stuff that was easy for me to earn and didn't take any effort. So I just spend a little money on you guys from the no-effort account! I have another account where I keep my hard-earned money. I won't touch that account, so you don't have to feel guilty."

Underneath Sam's humor is a very good point that should not be lost on people having their own business. And that is the whole reason you got into this business was because you didn't want everything in your life to be back-breaking struggle, with only incremental pay raises over the years. You wanted to get into a zone where the money started flowing more freely. There's nothing wrong with that, and that's really what this whole book is about: to teach you how that can happen for you.

"You guys really think I'll have enough money left to make this thing succeed?" Vern asks.

"Wrong question," says Sam.

"How's that?" asks Vern.

"Small business success is based on your will, not your wealth," Sam answers.

Lie #

I Don't Need Any Help

Lie number eight may be the most harmful of all. This lie has you thinking you should be able to do this on your own. It has you setting yourself up to fail. It has you insisting you've got what it takes. It has your ego and pride interfering with the success of your business.

But if you want success, you want your ego completely out of the picture. Rather than focusing on yourself and whether you've got what it takes to succeed, you want to focus on the *result* you want.

It's a matter of priorities.

You have to put the success of your business ahead of false pride. You have to put the success of your business ahead of whether you might "lose face" or look weak.

There's a basic principle here you should not ignore: What you focus on expands. Whatever you direct your attention to in your life expands and grows. So keep your eyes on the prize, and don't go it alone. If you are more committed to success than anything else, then you won't care at all how your success happens or how many people you'll share the credit with.

The paradoxical power of setting your ego aside and seeking help is that it suggests strength, not weakness. It means you are committed to an outcome. Most people are not fully committed to success; they are only committed to looking good in the eyes of others. They may be somewhat committed to making a living, but that's a completely different thing! If you are only committed to making a living, then that's the most your business will ever do for you. It will only give you a place inside of which you can try to make a living.

But is that why you went into this business? Wasn't there a bigger idea than that? Didn't you go into it because you saw the possibilities of having a great life, full of freedom and joy?

When you finally commit to success (to building a life, rather than making a living), you will get lots of help. It's as simple as that. (And the very fact that you are reading this book will tell you that you are already reaching out in that direction and therefore truly committed to success.)

In all walks of life, you can tell whether people are *committed* to something by whether they are getting help. Whether they are reaching out, free of ego, free of pride (and the paranoia that comes with pride) and *connecting* with someone who can help.

Tiger Woods uses a coach. When he got rid of his original coach, saying he could do it on his own, his game went downhill fast. Bob Nardelli, CEO of The Home Depot, has said, "I absolutely believe that people, unless coached, never reach their maximum capabilities."

Many of us have either directly experienced addiction recovery or have a friend or family member who has. The first step in recovery is knowing you need help. Without that, you are doomed. So many of our clients are addicted to these nine lies, addicted to misinformation and excuses and the temporary good feelings they get when other people confirm for them how hard success is, and how impossible it is to make it on your own in business.

Sam, who is often featured on national TV shows and known throughout his native Canada as "The Small Business Millionaire," talks openly about the five businesses he had that *failed* before he got this crucial message into his soul.

Sam finally took stock and realized he needed help! He realized he didn't have to do this small business thing alone. In fact, all the effort he was putting into doing it all on his own was working against him. Once Sam gave up being a loner and a hero, he discovered that the blueprint for small business success was already available to him. People had been there all along, ready to help him. They had written books for him about how they succeeded in their own businesses. They were giving their secrets away! They were willing to coach and consult. Sam just needed to make the commitment to drop the ego and reach out.

"I had tried to run my previous businesses on common sense," Sam said. "All of these nine falsehoods that undermine a business masquerade as common sense. But common sense was failing, and I was just sick of it. I remember one day thinking that *I simply will no longer fail.* No more failure. I will do whatever it takes now to succeed. Whatever it takes!"

And in that moment Sam dropped his ego out of the equation and looked for help. He realized that success was not a mystery. Success leaves clues. So Sam decided to find out how other people succeeded and let successful people teach him to succeed. He reached out. (You know you are committed to something when you reach out.)

Sam was sick of humiliation. He was even sick of the car he was driving! He was sick of the feeling he got each evening when he thought about his finances.

So he made his commitment.

"I started reading one, two, three books a week," Sam said. "I started going to the library to look at other people's Yellow Pages ads to see what successful businesses were doing in other cities. I started investing in knowledge, the knowledge I would use to make my business successful. I really got into it. I started attending seminars, I bought tapes for my car, I signed up for coaching! And all of this paid off. A lot of people have questioned me about the money I spent to get all this help, a lot of people have said, 'Well, that's a lot of money to spend on seminars and coaching and learning tools,' but compared to what our business now makes? It's a laugh. It's the best investment I ever made."

Sam was not in some kind of fancy, trendy, high-tech business when he did this. He and his wife owned a little dance studio! It's an industry that is notoriously cash-poor, wherein most studio owners believe that being financially strapped is just part of the package. If you love dance or music you are an artist, and if you are an artist you are probably a starving artist! Sam has completely reversed that stereotype and taught hundreds of others to reverse it, too.

Most small businesses fail because their owners are addicted to doing it on their own, to sinking or swimming, to waiting four years to be profitable, to fighting the good fight, to staying up late at night poring over the desperate books, to not taking vacations for fear that the business will go under while they are away, to feeling a kind of loneliness in their battle they haven't felt since the terrifying moments of early childhood when their mother first dropped them off at school, to making it a matter of pride and self-esteem to find the answers on their own, to trying to use common sense to make this business work when common sense keeps letting them down. They transform, day by day, from a person who was happy and optimistic about serving others into someone who is bitter and wary of untrustworthy customers.

Excuses for failure soon become an addiction! And as with any other addiction, you'll never recover until you ask for help.

Doug Would Do This on His Own, Thank You

Doug is the type of business owner we just described, struggling and fighting the good fight on his own, thinking he is proud and macho enough to face this thing all by himself, month in and month out.

Doug gets in his car. He wants a little distraction from his business stress, and so he flips on the radio. For the whole drive in to work he hears horror stories about disasters, crimes, and other people's problems. In some strange way it gives him some relief! *Some people have it worse than I do!*

Doug gets out of his car and takes a very deep breath because the business day has begun, and who knows what will be waiting for him? What creditor will be angry? What kind of employee crisis will present itself? Who hasn't showed up for work? Why were yesterday's receipts so low, especially in light of our increased ad spending? The list never ends, and no one knows how hard this is. Doug has become a victim of his business, and that very fact is what is keeping his business from expanding and succeeding. But Doug doesn't know. He thinks it's just real life. Just the reality about owning your own business.

"Hey!" says Doug. "That's why they call it work!"

Doug takes one brief moment before entering his store to look across the street. That young woman Miranda has a lot of nerve! Opening a competing business on the same street as Doug's! Well, wait until reality hits her. Wait until she feels the crunch of the economy around here. Wait until she sees how hard this market is to succeed in.

But what's that? Why is her parking lot filled, and why am I seeing all those people filing in and out of her business? What kind of price cut has she done? Is she insane, or just vicious? I can't afford to think about it.

Miranda's store is thriving today, but she herself hasn't physically showed up for work yet. She's in her car on her way back from a three-day weekend spent upstate at a beautiful resort, where she took a seminar on direct-mail advertising and other aggressive marketing techniques. In her car she is not listening to the radio or the news, but to her audio learning programs for growing her business. Miranda has a fresh set of CDs she bought online about turning a profit in your first year in business. The tapes are not only informative, filling Miranda with fresh ideas for her store, but they are entertaining, too! The author on the tape has a wry sense of humor and often has Miranda laughing about how and why so many businesses fail in their first year. It sinks in. Miranda makes a note to pass these CDs on to her employees.

Most people today waste all their drive time. They spend it either worrying about their own problems or taking refuge in talk radio and the news, so they can distract themselves with other people's problems. They curse the fates that never allowed them to get a decent education, especially in the crucial areas of business management and marketing, not realizing that *the best education in the world* is now available in audio. (See our Recommended Reading list at the back of this book.)

One of the most profound lessons is contained in Thomas Stanley's *The Millionaire Next Door* (itself an audio program worth purchasing). It is that most people who become millionaires in America are similar to Miranda and Sam. They are not in some tricky, trendy, high-tech business that catapults them to wealth overnight. On the contrary, most millionaires are in everyday, ordinary small businesses similar to yours, Miranda's, and Sam's. Tom Stanley's point is that although your business itself may be ordinary, your approach to it doesn't have to be. You yourself don't have to be ordinary.

We Had 200,000 Miles on Our Car

"'We had just gotten married when we started business number six," recalled Sam. "The wedding was actually pretty funny. We were broke, for one thing. We just had this one car, which was actually my wife Val's car before we got married and it was an old Honda with 200,000 miles on it. No one would have thought our prospects were very good. Especially if you saw us driving around in that beat-up car."

The year was 1995, and soon after the wedding Sam and Val found themselves sitting in a big seminar called "Success '95!"

"We were just sitting there listening to these speakers," Sam said, "and the last thing I felt like was successful, because our business lives had just been failure after failure after failure. My actual personal income as reported on my tax forms in 1994 was $0! Zero! I didn't make any money at all. I was borrowing money from friends just to live, and staying with people, and moving from place to place so I'd have a place to sleep. It was pretty bad."

But Sam stayed at the "Success 95" seminar, listened, and took notes. From there he began his journey to success by continuing to reach out for help outside his own ego.

Books, tapes, seminars, and coaching from people who know how to make a business successful became Sam's passionate quest.

"I decided I was not going to leave anything to chance this time," Sam said. "I was going to learn how to do this. And what I found, much to my delight, is that there is a way, a system, that anybody can use to succeed with. And it includes not going it alone. It includes always having someone coach you, some way, somehow, whether at live seminars, through teleseminars, or personal coaching, or Internet mastermind groups, or learning tools."

Sam also realized another value to getting outside help: *objectifying the business.* The more objective you can be when working on your business, the faster you will improve it. The more subjective you are—the more personal you make everything (the more the whole success/failure issue becomes about *you* instead of about your business)—the harder it is to succeed because it has become too personal. It has descended into those creepy psychological waters where you review your whole past history of self-esteem, parental psychological abuse (no matter how subtle), willpower, personal character flaws and personality defects, trust issues—the list becomes endless and severely depressing. You can't succeed with this approach!

The business has to be a thing that is *not you.* Something you can step back from and work on. Then it can really be improved! Don't focus on yourself, focus on the business. Would a surgeon want to lay some tools out on his kitchen table and sit down to give himself a vasectomy? (True story: We knew a doctor who actually did this to himself at his home after hearing a lot of yelling from his kids in the other room, but he later said that he did not recommend it.) Most surgeons go to other doctors for their surgery, because you are always more skillful working on something other than yourself.

"After my business failures I realized that I had to stop making the business be about me," Sam recalled. "If I was going to succeed, I knew I had to make the business bigger than myself. So I started getting coaching and consulting for that very reason. When there was an outside coach involved, our focus was on the business, not on me. So now you've got two people looking at the business and putting their brains together to move it forward. Like two people pushing a wagon, you get so much farther!"

With outside help, your business becomes a work of art. It's something you're designing and shaping. It's no longer something you're just tangled up in.

"It's like any kind of counseling," said Sam. "If you have any kind of issue and see a counselor for it, it allows you to step outside the problem and work on the problem. The counselor helps isolate the problem and tells you, 'okay we have identified this problem, and we're going to work on this problem and we're going to help you beat this problem.' Then you are no longer tempted to say *I am this problem.* You have creative distance and leverage that you never had when you couldn't separate yourself from the problem."

No professional athlete would dream of going a day without coaching. Because their success is too important to leave to chance. They wouldn't dream of going it alone.

Yet most small business owner are actually *proud* of going it alone! As if that said something good about them.

It does not. It says that they are not fully committed to success.

The great golfer Jack Nicklaus, after playing a bad round, would often go take some lessons from a local golf pro. How could a local golf pro give the great Nicklaus lessons? Because the golf pro could bring objectivity back into Jack's game, and the two of them could work on Jack's game, *not on Jack.* If Jack instead had made his bad round be about him, instead of just about his game, he might have plunged into a long "slump," worried to death about himself. This thing called success isn't about you. It's about your business.

Get Help From Your Own People

Your employees are a wonderful source of help for you, too. Especially if you insist on hiring good ones. Many business owners hire people haphazardly, just to fill an immediate need, and they end up having employee nightmares that keep them from the important aspects of their business growth.

For your business to really please the customer and grow with good prices and profit margins, your employees must be a reflection of you. They must be just as you are with the customer. They must understand deeply and fully the value of a lifelong customer versus a one-time hit, and they must be enrolled in the mission of getting lifelong customers who refer others.

So many small businesses break down right at this juncture. The business owner may understand how to please customers but hires a moody receptionist to work at the front desk with the customers, and the customers become frustrated and annoyed. Or the owner might hire employees who are bad on the phone and don't make customers feel welcome when they call. All the best-laid plans can go up in smoke because one employee is having a bad day.

Hire good, friendly, happy people. Just do it. Insist on it. (They will help you succeed.) And when you make a mistake and get someone in who does not represent your business well, do not hesitate to replace him or her. It's not the people you fire who give you problems—it's the people you don't fire.

Remember: You need help. You can't be the only committed person in your business. Make sure your employees are helping you succeed every moment of the day.

Make sure your hiring process gives you a competitive advantage. How? Any creative way you can do it, but a good rule of thumb is to pay more attention to the hiring process than your competitor does. That's a good place to start. Then, spend more time interviewing than your competition does. You will never regret spending lots of time interviewing, because getting one great employee in there can make a huge difference in your business's fortunes, *especially if that employee interacts with your customer.*

The are two reasons to spend a good deal of time interviewing prospective employees:

1. If the prospect is not the right fit for the customer relations you want to create, you

will start getting red flags in the interview. (The longer the interview, the more certain you are that something in your gut is telling you no! The length of the interview increases the accuracy of your intuition.)

2. If this person is a good fit for your team, the longer you interview, the more sure you will become. In hiring, length of interview alone is a major competitive advantage.

Now that you've got good employees hired, it's time to help them help you. Share the vision, and share the strategy with them. Let them fully realize what it is that makes your business worth more than the competition. Get them so fully grounded in the value you are offering that they become unconscious salespeople to everyone they talk to. Let them help you with ideas, too. Meet with them often and ask for their creative thinking on how the customer can be even more pleased.

These activities might seem obvious, but to many they are not. Most small businesses descend into an adversarial relationship with the customer. The business manager has to deal with upset customers and so he shares his frustration with his employees, who pick the theme up and run with it: "Customers are a hassle! They are demanding and cheap. They will try to rip you off! We love it, *love* it, when we get a break and things quiet down and there aren't so many of them coming in. Whew, what a respite. What a godsend this day has been! Almost no one came in. Yesterday we were slammed! Totally slammed!"

Your employees want to help make the business successful, but they have to know what the game is. You define the game. Let them be co-owners of your business, fully partnered professionals in the art of pleasing and adding value to customers. If that's your game, that will be their game.

When employees treat customers badly, it originates in careless hiring practices, but it gets perpetuated by the owner. The employees take their cue from the owner. So you must model for them, day in and day out, how to treat each customer. And you must coach them, too, so that they know what the objective is. The objective is not to just get through the day of work and get the paycheck. The objective is to please the customer in extraordinary and unforgettable ways that will prompt referrals. Get everyone on that page and get everyone thinking in those terms, and your employees will really help you grow the business.

Asking for Help Is a Sign of Strength

Roman had a little ad agency of his own that had run into deep debt. One of his major clients had unexpectedly gone under, leaving him with huge bills to pay and no income from that client. In addition to that, Roman had been trying to go it alone, never realizing how bad he was at running a business.

"I was great at creating ads," said Roman. "My work was the most creative in town and a lot of people were impressed and wanted me to do their advertising. I was just clueless about the other part of business, though. The part of business that is referred to as running a business."

Soon Roman's business debts were so great that he was facing bankruptcy. Why did other, less-talented people make it in advertising in his small town? What was wrong with him?

"I actually went into psychotherapy," said Roman. "I was so depressed about running my business into the ground that I knew it had to be about me. Some huge defect in me. Then, one day, my therapist said, 'Why don't you get some help?' And I literally didn't know what she meant. My father never would have needed help. Is that even American to ask for help?"

Roman found a retired accountant named Walter living in his town and asked Walter if he would come in, on an hourly fee, and help. Walter's fee was small because he just relished the idea of getting back into business. He hated retirement, and when he looked at Roman's books he saw an enormous challenge. After a full week of study, he asked for a meeting with Roman.

"We are going to climb out of this debt and we are going to make this business strong," said Walter.

"But how?" said Roman, who was long past hope.

"By asking for help," said Walter.

"Oh, that won't work," said Roman. "The banks have given up on us. We can't get any more loans."

"That's not what I mean," said Walter. "I mean our creditors. Our vendors. We are going to ask for their help. I have a plan worked out. We are going to pay them, but at a much slower, lower pace than they are demanding. We will ask them to help us save the business by giving us two years instead of 90 days to pay them. But we will pay them regularly."

"What if they won't do it?" asked Roman.

"I will meet with each one myself," said Walter. "I will have their first check in my hand. They can sign the two-year agreement and take the check, or not. If not, I will not give them the check. They can take us to court, but they will know that their case in court will not be a good one because we have already made them a pay-back offer in good faith."

Roman was amazed but allowed Walter to carry out his plan. Remarkably, not one of the vendors objected. In fact, some of them called Roman thanking him for taking the time to meet with them and create such a thorough plan!

"I never dreamed these vendors would help me," said Roman. "I had begun to think of them as enemies. People out to torture and humiliate me."

Roman called me last year asking for career coaching, even though his creative consulting business was thriving.

"Why do you think you need coaching?" I asked him. "What would you use it for? It seems like you are already doing quite well."

"I want to go somewhere I've never gone before," said Roman. "I keep having this funny feeling that there is a level of success out there that I haven't even imagined. And I'm also tired of all the traveling I do. I've read your books, and they struck a chord. So I created an ideal scene wherein I travel less, work less, and make twice as much. For this, I need your help."

Roman had realized an important small business truth: The stronger you are, the more help you'll ask for.

Help is everywhere. Your vendors want to help you succeed. Your employees are a fantastic source of help. Your customers will help you if you let them. Talk to them! They'll tell you how to improve.

And seek out other successful people. Let them teach you how they did it. It is not all that complicated. But it starts with reaching out. It starts with abandoning your ego. This isn't about your ego. It's about the success of your business!

You can check out *www.smallbusinesstruth.com*, but check other coaching and mastermind group options also. You can download free articles as a purchaser of this book because we value you as our customer, and we hope you like what you've read so far. The point is to reach out and not leave your success to chance. Have someone else commit to it along with you. That's the ultimate value of a coach or consultant: their commitment to your success. Add that to their objectivity and daily positive experience engineering success for others like you and you are on your way. You can get help from us or someone else, but the point is that you accelerate your success if you get help from somewhere.

You don't have to do this by yourself. And you don't have to be like Sam and have five businesses fail before you wake up, as he did, to the truth that says: *To ask for help is to be committed to success.*

Lie

I Am a Victim of Circumstance

The ninth lie is the one that makes all the other lies possible: the lie I tell to myself that paints me as a victim of circumstance.

Business owners fall into this trap constantly.

One of our clients, and we'll call her Misty, has a franchise store, and she attends yearly meetings of all the franchise owners. And though many of their sessions are about strategies for growing their businesses, most of the talk at the meetings is about negative circumstances.

"The other owners and I would get together between meetings, at lunch, and after the sessions out at restaurants and bars, and we would talk about all the negative stuff we were faced with," Misty recalled. "We'd confirm our worst fears for each other. We'd talk about how hard it is to find good staffing help. We'd talk about how bad the economy has been for our product, how brutal the competition has become, why the media are harder to trust for advertising, and it would go on for hours. Our yearly meetings should have had suicide hotlines and grief counselors on standby, because they always became meetings about the problems we face with all these circumstances we can't control."

When Misty signed up for some of our coaching the first thing we had to do was get her to spew out all the lies her fellow franchise-owners were unwittingly perpetuating about the business they were in. It was ugly. It was similar to a scene from *The Exorcist*. It was clear that Misty had given all her power away, and that her "colleagues" were supporting her in feeling helpless.

Why do they do this? Why do they deepen the psychological damage for each other? Maybe it's because this lie that says that "we are victims of circumstance" gives the franchisees a form of short-term comfort. It is an almost-tranquilizing experience of victimization and a sense that there are powers at play that are rendering fresh action impossible. How sad, but what a relief!

But what they didn't see was that it was all made up. There was no truth to what they were saying to each other.

During our de-programming of Misty, it almost felt as if she had been captured by a cult and we had to get her back into normal society. We had to wash her brain back to normal by giving her a fresh dose of small business truth.

"I had truly begun to believe that *I had no power* to affect outcomes in my store," said Misty. "What I had to re-learn was that I could use the law of cause and effect to make my business prosperous. I could cause things."

You Are the Maker of Your Circumstance

If you have been telling yourself that you can't *cause* your success to happen, then you *are* a victim, but not a victim of circumstance, a victim of your own thinking.

So, let's introduce a useful distinction: It just might be possible that all small business managers are separated into two camps: victims and owners. This is a concept first introduced my book *Reinventing Yourself* (about how people reinvent themselves from victims to owners) and later taught in my live seminars to more than 30 Fortune 500 corporations.

The good news is that people, once they see this distinction, can change very quickly. The good news is that they don't have to be a victim for one minute more.

"I thought I was stuck with my underperforming employees," said Misty. "I knew there was something wrong with having them work for me, but when I went to our annual meetings, other owners would say, 'Tell me about it!' and then we would try to top each others' bad employee stories."

Soon Misty put some performance measurement systems into her store. She started keeping score and giving rewards. And, as we predicted, the poorer performers complained.

"They were really offended that I would put the sales standings up in the back office in such large print," said Misty. "One of them came to me one morning and said she didn't appreciate coming to work and seeing herself in *last place* in the standings each morning. She asked me, 'How am I supposed to deal with that first thing in the morning?' I suggested that *selling something* would be a way. She left the conversation in a huff and quit the next week. The person I hired to replace her is wonderful and loves being ranked according to how she's doing. I never knew I could do any of this."

Misty is similar to most small business owners: She had no idea how much power she had to change the results she was getting in her business. She had given all her power away to circumstance.

As you look back on your business so far, you will see that you always have had two basic ways of being. At any given time, you were either one way, or you were the other. You were either being an owner of your outcomes, or you were being a victim of circumstances. And the choice was always yours.

One way, the ownership way, reinvented you as you confronted the circumstance. It always grew you up. Was a certain customer complaining? You took complete ownership of the situation and grew with it. It gave you ideas for future customers. Soon, you avoided nothing. Everything and everyone was your teacher. You realized that you finally understood what the Dalai Lama meant when he said, "My enemy is my greatest teacher."

You used each "negative" circumstance as a teacher or a weight to make you smarter or stronger. Choosing that way of thinking reinvented you outward, in an ever-expanding circle of compassion, vision, and courage.

But when you chose the other way (the victim way), it would always shrink your power down to nothing. Just as your muscles shrink when they are not used, so do your heart and soul when you are repeatedly choosing the victim mode. You lose heart. Your business looks too hard to master.

Choose to Really Own Your Business

When we are choosing to be owners, we give all of ourselves to what we're doing at any given moment. We pour all our energy into the current moment's task. We notice that when we give ourselves fully to something, we own it. In a sense, we wrap our spirit around it completely.

If an employee wants to talk to us, we focus fully and completely on that talk. That very talk might create a break-through for the business! If a customer has a complaint, we own it. We become fascinated and curious about it. We realize that it is going to teach us something very important.

Bill Gates had a small business that he built into Microsoft. He makes certain the Microsoft employees stop and study every customer complaint. "Your most *unhappy customers* are your greatest source of learning," Gates said.

The paradox of creating a great future for our business is that it always takes place in the present moment. This little task right here in front of me will have more to do with my future than any series of worries I may string together.

"Don't waste life in doubts and fears," said Ralph Waldo Emerson. "Spend yourself on the work before you, well-assured that the right performance of this hour's duties will be the best preparation for the hours and ages that will follow it."

And almost every truly happy business owner we know has somewhere along the way learned to separate happiness from pleasure—and know that they are not at all similar. In most ways they are opposites! Pleasure is short term and happiness is long term.

Or, as radio talk show host Dennis Prager said: "What most people lack are: (1) the awareness that what will make them happy demands a great deal of thought, and (2) the self-discipline to overcome their natural inclination to do what is most pleasurable at the moment instead of what is most happiness-inducing."

Victims take the opposite approach. If an employee needs to talk to a victim employer, the employer rolls his eyes upward and agrees resentfully, and during the talk takes two cell calls, checks his computer twice for e-mail alerts, and calls out over the employee's shoulder to another person, giving the impression that, *I never had time for this talk with you.* Even though that talk, if paid attention to, would have grown the business.

Victims Miss 100 Opportunities a Day for Growing the Business

I had a client in Indiana who invited me to do a daylong series of one-on-one talks with his seven employees. One of the questions I asked each person I talked to was, "If you owned this business, what would you do right now to make it better?"

It was amazing how many good ideas I got. I took a lot of the ideas to the owner, who listened to me and took notes. Many of these ideas are in place in the business today, and the business is better for it. The owner thinks I'm a genius, but I just listened.

A victim is someone who always sees power as something beyond his or her control. It belongs to the banks. It belongs to competitors. It's in the whimsical hands of untrustworthy customers. Victims have a habitually pessimistic way of viewing and describing the world and its people. And although this victimization can often last a lifetime, it is only a habit. When it's understood, it can be quickly replaced.

> **Small business truth:**
> *Habits are not broken; they're replaced.*

Victims do not get their habit from heredity. They *think themselves* into it. And then, as in the case of Misty, they get support from other victims. Soon their lies feel like the truth. And what is tragic is that their thinking is based on a fundamental misunderstanding, a misunderstanding that is as fundamental as thinking that the world is flat. Victims think all power lies outside of his or herself. Victims then continue this misperception by thinking and speaking in deeply pessimistic terms about everything they are challenged by. Not only is the situation difficult, but it *makes them* depressed, angry, sad, or frustrated. Soon victims are easily discouraged. One ad doesn't work, or one person quits or calls in sick, and the victim mind is experiencing a chain reaction. Soon all that day's tasks and opportunities for growth are met with less energy. Less creativity. Less hope. Less enthusiasm. Less power and effectiveness. Soon nothing seems to work.

When victims come to our seminars they talk about their business history, and their stories take on the weary tones of people who are always living in the past. They seem to have little energy for anything. We don't understand him or her. Things are different in their market! Their business is unique (and he or she is *uniquely cursed*). Soon, his or her passive tendency to fall into depression reminds us of André Gide's observation that "sadness is almost always a form of fatigue." This sadness is heartbreaking because it is so unnecessary.

Victims begin to recover when they allow themselves to know this truth: Small business is a game. Good things start to happen once victim wakes up to this.

"One of the insights I got into my fellow franchise owners was that they didn't really believe in business as a positive concept," said Misty during a recent coaching session.

"Tell me what you mean by that," I said.

"Well, they all talked about money and business and profit as if the whole thing were somehow fundamentally corrupt as an idea," she said. "I found myself disagreeing, but I didn't say anything. They seemed to think that they would be better off in some kind of massive government-run commune. It was as if they were completely unaware of world history."

Many people concluded after the Enron scandal (and the following scandals that sent some top business executives to jail) that there must be something wrong with the "free market economy" or "capitalism." That was a typical victim's response, an attempt to take the spotlight off of personal responsibility and put it on something vague and menacing that's victimizing us all. But what was really to blame in these scandals was the behavior of *individual* criminals and unethical business people. They were specific human beings. The more we generalized away from those human beings and made it "the system's" fault, the less accountable future individuals would need to feel.

It is of no service to the psyche of the small business owner that our media and educational systems continuously demonize and denigrate "the profit motive" and capitalism. It's hard to enthuse yourself about doing something that is generally regarded as greedy and immoral.

That's why so many small business owners benefit by joining groups of positively like-minded people. We say "positively" because if it's a group such as Misty's franchise group, it's not a benefit. Most groups are not like that. They have to be truly devoted to sharing the magic.

Some small business owners form mastermind groups, join industry associations, attend local business breakfast events, and enroll in coaching programs and Websites such as our own to take back the night. They want to take back that spirit that surged through North America in the 1930s and 1940s, that spirit of free enterprise and unlimited personal achievement.

I once had a small marketing business of my own many years ago. A major breakthrough occurred for me when I joined an association of other businesses similar to mine. We met twice a year, and our group leader was so powerful and creative that all our businesses got charged up from the meetings. We shared stuff that worked. We learned to be owners and not victims.

True owners take full responsibility for their business success. They even take responsibility for their energy levels, whatever they may be. They continuously tap into the power of the human spirit. They use that spirit as a fire to invent, and then reinvent, who they are. They don't look for lucky breaks to supply their excitement. They're not waiting for deliverance. They don't wish they were somewhere else. They agree with author Nathaniel Branden that "*this earth* is the distant star we must find a way to reach."

A Wild Thing Will Make Your Heart Sing

Victim employers repeatedly make the mistake of talking to their own employees about how hard things are. Recently we worked with a small organization wherein the leader, whom we will call Nick, spent a good part of his meetings with his employees reminding them what pressures the business was under. He wanted their help, but the only way he knew to ask for their help was to approach them as a martyr.

"We're under a lot of pressure right now," Nick said in the company meeting we attended. "We're behind schedule and a lot of people—bankers, vendors, and creditors—are all expecting a lot of things from us. And as everyone knows, this isn't the easiest business to be in. This is also the tough season we're entering into, and the local economy is—well, we'll get through this crisis. I'm sure of it!"

It was easy to see that Nick was that group's biggest problem. When Nick met with us after the meeting we told him so.

"You're the biggest thing this company has to overcome," I told him. "It isn't any of the pressures you listed in your meeting. It's you, Nick. Your company has a big problem, and it's you. But there's good news here. Because you're the problem, you're the solution."

Nick worked with us carefully over the next few months to completely reinvent who he was. Instead of being a fellow victim, he emerged as a leader. The more he *owned* his business, the more inspiring he became.

Over the years Sam and I have found out that people will show the boss some sympathy when he pities himself, but they don't necessarily look forward to talking to him that much.

The great and spirited novelist D.H. Lawrence said, "I never saw a wild thing sorry for itself. A small bird will drop frozen dead from a bough without ever having felt sorry for itself." That's because wild things live lives of pure action. Today, the more you as a business owner live as a "wild thing," taking action instead of meditating on your sad condition, the faster self-pity melts away, and the more people want to help you. Your high energy will put you at a vibratory level that attracts people's help. People want to help people who are enthusiastic, not people who are down in the dumps. You're going to motivate your people more from a surge of mad joy than from sadness.

Remember the words of André Gide: "Sadness is almost never anything but a form of fatigue." And fatigue, paradoxically, is almost always a result of living a life of too little action. The more action you build into your business, the better you sleep. The better you sleep, the more energy you have. The more energy you have, the more will you have for taking action, and the more action you take, the happier you feel. The happier you feel, the better your professional relationships. People and customers are drawn to happy people.

Helen Keller also offered her insight into the human condition with the following: "No pessimist ever discovered the secrets of the stars, or sailed to an uncharted land, or opened a new heaven to the human spirit." Keller, who was deaf and blind, saw no justification for pessimism or playing the victim. She was blind, but not a victim. She was deaf, but not a victim. Can your small business challenges be justification enough?

The real problem with voicing your pessimism to your employees, vendors, and families is that it shuts down their brains. To hear it constantly can be likened to shutting down your computer when you need it the most.

Optimism opens the brain up to more and more possibilities. That's the function of optimism. Optimism isn't just shallow, smiling euphoria. It runs deep into the most creative parts of the brain and helps solve problems faster and generate fresh plans of action. Or, as the award-winning Dr. Martin Seligman stated in his book *Learned Optimism* (Knopf, 1998):

> Why should we bother to learn to think optimistically? Isn't pessimism just a posture with no real effects? Unfortunately not. I have studied pessimism for the last 20 years, and in more than one thousand studies, involving more than half a million children and adults, pessimistic people do worse than optimistic people in three ways: First, they get depressed much more often. Second, they achieve less at school, on the job and on the playing field, much less than their talents would suggest. Third, their physical health is worse than that of optimists. So holding a pessimistic theory of the world may be the mark of sophistication, but it is a costly one.

And that's the interesting thing about these nine lies. All of these lies are lies of sophistication. They allow the speaker to seem cool when mixing with other negative, sophisticated pessimists. Being excited about the future has never been seen as sophisticated in our society. But it grows businesses.

What About Hurricanes and Cancer?

Three years ago, a lovely woman (and one of Sam's clients) named Marty Simon was diagnosed with what was thought to be terminal breast cancer. And when she was going through chemotherapy she found it hard to stay interested in growing her business.

However, when Marty had her surgery, she could only take three days off to recover, because she couldn't afford to be away from her little music studio for any longer than that. She and her husband Ross had started with 43 students, and that was how it held for several years. Things were difficult. Money was scarce. And they actually qualified for food stamps, but never took advantage of it. It was a struggle. The two of them did everything: They taught all the music lessons themselves, they cleaned the studio themselves, they called parents, they answered the phone, they signed people up. It was all done by Marty and Ross.

They had started their business in an 800-square-foot building that was thought of as a high-rise in Cape Coral, Florida. They were on the second floor, and a spooky stairwell led up to their studio. You could see the duct tape on the floor that had been there for about five years.

"Our landlord was also very interesting," recalled Marty. "He decided to put carpeting on the walls so we wouldn't disturb the eight other businesses that were around us. So we had a lovely gray carpeted look all the way through the studio. At one point, one of the ladies left a lit cigarette in the ladies' room and burned up the ladies room, and the landlord didn't get around to fixing it for two years."

"Here we were in steamy, sweltering southwest Florida, and for two years we had no airconditioning! And when you're trying to give a voice lesson to a student and saying, 'Just breathe,' and it's 95 degrees in the room, it gets very exciting. So we were stuck."

And although these facts would tempt almost anyone to fall for the victim lie, Marty and Ross remained cheerful and upbeat, learning everything they could from everything life threw at them and seeing everything as a lesson designed to strengthen their way. They had a sense that they were on a path, but they didn't yet know where it was leading.

So Marty and Ross kept trying to save money here and there, but it kept looking as if they were stuck with no sign of growth for their little business.

"As Sam Beckford says, we were saving ourselves into the poor house," said Marty, looking back on those days. "No money to advertise, nothing. But when the student is ready, the teacher appears. And for some reason God chose to heal me, and at the same time we believe that He also chose for us to look at Sam's advertisement instead of throwing it away. Which I'm sure we had done the past few years before. So when we got the advertisement, we decided to go for it, mostly because we had no chance to do anything else, and we were desperate."

So Marty and Ross wrote down three goals. Their first goal was to double their customer base from 43 to 86 students. The second was to find a larger space to rent, preferably with airconditioning. And the third was to spend less time teaching, so they could actually be away from the business and have it still run efficiently. They had no money at all, of course, so they had to get creative to even find a way to get to Sam's seminar!

But once a person takes *owner*ship, the world shifts, too.

So Marty and Ross used frequent flyer miles to pay for their plane ticket and then they rummaged around the house and found $500 in traveler's checks that had been left over from a trip 10 years before, and they cashed those in. Then they also found 30 Canadian dollars from a trip 10 years before, and so they got to Vancouver and paid for the hotel.

"Of course, the seminar was awesome, and when we returned we were anxious to get started," said Marty. "The first thing we did was change our name from Simon Music Studios to Cape Coral Academy of Music. This would take our names out of the business, and Sam had said if you name your business for the area, it just feels like you've been there longer. And it worked. We found a larger building. And this was key. We actually were able to negotiate free rent for the month of July for the next three years with our landlord. And that strategy, which we learned from Sam, paid for our seminar three times over, so we were very excited about that. It actually worked!"

Then they started a new kind of advertising. It was advertising that actually attracted customers, instead of just getting their name out. Ross was very good with desktop publishing, so he did all of the artwork. He used to be a professional photographer, so he was able to do everything that they used in their advertising. They also added a 24-hour info line. They applied many tips and ideas they learned from other attendees at the seminar.

When you give up being a victim and completely flush that thinking out of your mind, all kinds of energy swells up to take its place. All kinds of fresh ideas for creating a successful customer base flood your mind.

At the seminar, Ross and Marty heard other business owners answer the question, "If you only had $1,000 to spend, how would you best spend it?" They heard Sam talk about the successful use of "door hangers."

"Well this was the first of our challenges," Ross said. "Because we found out there was a city ordinance against door hangers."

But challenges only defeat victims. They energize owners.

"Then we had some personal challenges," said Marty. "Two weeks before our scheduled opening, my mother—and I'm an only child—was diagnosed with terminal cancer. On moving day, my mother was admitted to the hospice. So some of our friends rallied around and gave me the greatest gift of a few more hours with my mother so that Ross could move the business, and I could be with Mom. On what was supposed to be our opening day, my mother passed away. We went to Pennsylvania for the burial, and a week after we returned, our house was robbed and they stole, among other things, our laptop, which had all of our studio artwork and studio records on it."

At this point, even many people who had been owners might want to go back to being a victim. But not Ross and Marty.

"If I sound like Job, it gets better!" laughed Marty, looking back on their earlier days. "This has a happy ending, not an unhappy ending. Basically, what we did was every time we had a challenge, we knew we had to regroup and start over. So we relied on our faith."

Soon they decided to join their chamber of commerce to coordinate their new opening day, which turned out to be in November, with a ribbon-cutting ceremony. They decided to make it into a formal ceremony. They had a pastor give an invocation, and they sent out invitations to that. They served food and had face-painting for the kids, and they also had all the music teachers get together for a jam session at the end of the night. That kept the crowd there and created a lot of interest.

The chamber arranged for the photo of the ribbon-cutting to appear in the paper—and it also appeared in their magazine. And that was totally free. They also arranged for Ross and Marty to be interviewed by the local paper and have a photo that appeared with it. So that gave them a jump-start in publicity. But the challenges weren't over yet.

Their next challenge was Hurricane Charlie. When the news of its impending disaster came, Ross and Marty had to get to a shelter, fast. And what was going through their minds when they went over to the shelter was, "Oh no, we could lose everything!" They packed a lot of their instruments in the car and took them with them. They figured they had a better chance at the shelter because their neighborhood was supposed to be flooded, and their house was perched along the water beside a little canal. Still, they were more concerned about the business than their house because the house was insured, but, as Marty said, "it's really hard to insure every single little piece of equipment in a business when you don't have much money to start with."

Because all the shelters were filled up, their little town had turned the high school into a shelter, and there were 5,000 people on two floors. They were pushing Coke machines against the doors because the force of Charlie was blowing the doors in! The power never went off because they had a generator, but soon all the bathrooms stopped working.

"We actually didn't leave for the shelter until it got really bad, because it went from a category 2 to a category 4 in 30 minutes," said Marty. "So we were going to ride it out at home, and then all of a sudden they said, 'Southwest Florida, get out now!'

Marty and Ross had their car full of instruments outside.

"I had two classical guitars that were in the car and a violin that belonged to Ross, and a trumpet, a flute, a bass guitar," Marty said. "So we just picked out as many of the instruments as we could find that would help us make a living when we got through with this and put them in the car."

Then, almost as fast as it started, it was over. They left the shelter and went home. They didn't visit their business until the next morning.

"We were really scared to drive over there," said Marty. "We were afraid of what we might find."

"Or might not find!" Ross said.

But, fortunately, even though part of the building that connects to Ross and Marty's business lost its roof, and even though the building across the street was totally devastated, their little business was just fine.

Marty stood up in front of her mastermind business group recently and reported the latest: "This year, our challenges were four hurricanes in five weeks," she said to a group who had never seen or experienced even one such event. "Many of the students' homes were damaged, and they had to take time off to get their lives back together. So we lost revenue because of that. We also had three more hurricane warnings and every time we had one, we had to dismantle six rooms, put everything in one room, get it up off the floor, and cover it with tarps. So by the fourth hurricane, we were getting a little tired of that. But we just kept on going."

One of the reasons Ross and Marty kept on going was because their business was now successful, and they *owned* the cause of that. They themselves had caused it, not fate or circumstance. They had gone from 40 students to 186 regular students! They had also gone from doing everything themselves, with two teachers, to employing nine teachers and a master office assistant running the day-to-day operations.

Marty stood in front of her stunned group (many of whom were discarding their own victim stories on the spot). She finished her story by saying, "We continue to study and learn, we've tested everything, and we've picked the brains of the other mastermind members. I'm going to show you a slide that tells you what we live by: *We are hard-pressed on every side, but not crushed. Perplexed, but not in despair. Persecuted, but not abandoned. Struck down, but not destroyed.* This is what we live by, and it's served us well."

Later Marty talked about other people in her life who have chosen to invest all of their mental energy in their victim stories.

"I've watched so many people make excuses," she said. "And excuses, to me, just mean it's not going to happen. And so you just don't really need to be doing that because it doesn't help; it doesn't do any good. It destroys your momentum."

Ross likened learning to succeed at business to learning to play a piece of music.

"When somebody has a piece of music that they're learning and they say, 'I can't do this,' I say, 'Well, as long as you keep that attitude up, you'll never learn it.'"

"I mean, we don't have kids of our own," Marty said, "so it's very important to us to have spiritual children for whom we are setting a good example, and we're letting them see that this kind of attitude works and this way of thinking can create success, whether it's in music or just in life, in general."

Ross and Marty now teach children more than just music. Whether they know it or not, they now also teach ownership. Because all their students and all their clients see their growth and success. They see the new building, the expansion, and the energy that success brings. They see people who could have quit at any stage in their journey and no one would have blamed them. Cancer? Hurricanes? Who would have blamed them for quitting and getting "real jobs"?

And that's the beauty of the choices they made, the choices that came from owning their lives instead of playing victims of circumstance. They reflect the inherent beauty in small business itself: the challenge. It's the ultimate challenge! To own and run your own business! There is nothing like it. And because it is the highest of adventures, it contains the ultimate risk: You could lose it.

An owner sees that as energizing. A victim sees that as paralyzing. And how do *you* choose to see it? Notice that we're saying, "How to you *choose* to see it?" We are not asking, "How do you see it?" The choice is the important part of this, and the most important part of all the consulting and work we do: getting you in touch with the choice.

Because most people don't see it as a choice. They hear the story of Ross and Marty and they think that there was "character," "will," "strong personalities," or some other permanent characteristic built into Ross and Marty from the start. This is not true! There were moments when Ross and Marty had no hope! They were ready to quit! But they chose not to.

You have the same choice they do. You do not have to have *any* of your business's success depend on your personality or character, your past history, or your strengths and weaknesses. You can create success based on your own conscious choices. Because it truly is. It is a *lie* that you are a helpless victim of circumstances. You are an owner of the power to choose. In the face of a circumstance, you can choose any response you want. You are not bound by your personality or past history. You have freedom. You can choose.

Approximately 90 percent of the circumstances our clients tell us about are nothing compared to being diagnosed with cancer or having a hurricane hit their business. So it's not even the circumstance that matters, it's the way they *chose* to deal with it. True ownership is awareness of choice. Victimization is surrendering choice to the circumstance. Why give the circumstances in your life all that power? Why not give the same power to yourself?

Dare to Create Something Great

Marty and Ross are lucky that they get to interact with children all day. To an owner, children are always worth observing because children love and enjoy the planet they are on. Children reinvent themselves continuously. We can hear their spirit in the air. We have only to open the window a little bit to hear the shouts of joy at the schoolyard down the road.

In a grown-up place of business, the shouts of joy are usually nowhere to be heard. Where did they go? They got replaced by victim stories.

But you can bring that joy back, just as Ross and Marty did, in the face of so many circumstances. Recall that joy that used to hit you in childhood. Bring it into your business. Because without joy, the ideas in this book won't be sustained. Not in the long run. You may get some short jolts of profit from this book, but in the long run your success will depend on the ownership you take of the way you create a joyful experience. Your decision to generate an enthusiastic approach to your business will be the most important decision you ever made, even more important than your decision to go into business.

Take a Walk on the Wild Side

Sometimes we'll share the following excerpt with our clients. It's from Deepak Chopra's *The Book of Secrets*:

Imagine a baby who wants to walk but has these reservations:

1. I don't want to look bad.
2. I don't want to fall down.
3. I don't want anyone else to watch me fail.
4. I don't want to live with the burden of failure.
5. I don't want to expend all my energy.
6. I don't want any pain.
7. I want to get things over as fast as possible.

We love sharing what Chopra has identified here, as he writes about how uncommitted we can be to mastery. We laugh at the idea that a baby would consider any of these seven ideas. We know that a baby would never walk if he did so. What is required for walking is total commitment, without any of these self-imposed limitations.

If you have an area of your business where you know you are not totally masterful but want to be, then the answer is to take it on as you did when you learned to walk. Take on your work without any of those seven reservations, and you will know what it is to own your work, without reservation. Ownership leads to joy, absolute, exhilarating joy. There is nothing like it. Watch a baby's face when he is first walking. Try for that in your work.

Own Every Moment of Time

When you choose to be a true owner, your time is what you own. Your own personal time is what you value the most in any given day.

"Since I calculated the true value of one hour of my time I have never washed my car by hand," Sam said. "I figured that if I can make more in one hour than it costs me to pay someone to wash my car, then I can literally 'create' time very cheaply. Time is the new money, and I'm looking to increase my time portfolio any way I can."

Similarly, Sam coaches his clients to see each day as a precious inventory of time and each moment as a powerful unit of energy. This is energy that can be directed either to high-return activities (working on growing your revenues, for example) or low-return activities (such as fighting fires and solving minor problems). It is a question of boldness. It is a question of being ruthless with your schedule. A question of not being a victim.

Sam started visiting a new car detailing shop that rented a service bay from the gas station about five minutes from his house. He took all three of his cars there regularly for the last year. The owner was a nice fellow who would do extra touches on Sam's cars at no charge and was usually able to fit him in on short notice.

"The first time I visited him he gave me a car wash customer card, kind of like a spin on the Subway sandwich cards you collect stamps on for a free sub," said Sam. "I thought that this guy was pretty sharp, because the card was a tool to encourage repeat business. Over the winter I stopped driving my convertible, and my other cars didn't get that dirty so I started just driving through the automatic car wash at any gas station that had one."

In the spring when his convertible was back on the road, Sam stopped by the same shop for a detail. He saw a handwritten poster board on the service bay that read:

> **BUSINESS CLOSED,**
> **EQUIPMENT FOR SALE.**
> **CALL RICHARD**
> **480-892-6290**

What had happened? Richard might say he was a victim of the "slow season," but we don't think that is what made his business fail. Richard thought he was doing great marketing by his "frequent customer card," but he actually wasn't.

"I never got a call or a postcard from Richard during the slow season," Sam remembered. "Richard must have thought that if I really wanted a car wash, I would come in on my own. But in my life, I actually do very few things 'on my own.' I get up in the morning by using an alarm clock, or by my wife giving me some gentle persuasion. I don't get all of my taxes filed until my accountant calls me (usually twice) to tell me what needs to be sent in. Most people don't take actions or make decisions 'on their own.' If Richard would have phoned me or 50 other customers that have spent over $500 last year on car detailing and gave us a reason to do business, the slow season would have had no effect on him. Or, how about a 'take your car in and your neighbor comes for free day,' just for the best customers? How about the 'year of car washes' Christmas gift certificate he could have sold by sending out a simple mail piece to a few of his customers? How about going to local neighboring businesses when the shop had no customers and offering the 'drop your car off at lunch and have it clean by the end of the day' event? No waiting, no hassle! There were all kinds of things Richard could have done had he taken ownership."

When you decide once and for all that you will be an owner of your business and its success, which is to say that you will take *full responsibility* for attracting customers, then ideas will flow, as they did for Sam when he thought of how he would have made Richard's business successful.

In the book *Start Small Finish Big,* a book that chronicles the business growth of Subway sandwiches, the founder Fred Deluca tells how the owner of a Subway franchise in Nebraska grew his store from $2,000 per week to $8,000 per week in just eight months.

The owner Todd Carpenter would work making sandwiches at lunchtime, and then in the afternoon he would go out door to door in the local neighborhood. He would say "Hi, I'm Todd. I own the Subway on Main Street." If they had never been to the store before Todd would give them a coupon for a free sandwich. If they had been to the store before, then Todd would give them a coupon for a two-for-one sandwich and would tell them to come with a friend. The results were fantastic, and this type of Open Hand thinking that worked for Todd could work for any type of business that has the potential of repeat sales, especially Richard's car wash!

Instead of closing permanently to shut down the business, Richard could have copied Todd from Subway and just closed down two hours a day to get out there and get customers. Instead he chose to be a victim. To him, it was being a victim of the seasonal nature of his business. But it doesn't matter what you are a victim *of*; if you are a victim, you are a victim. (Marty had cancer, but she was not a cancer *victim*.)

Some business owners are afraid to contact previous customers because they don't want to "bug" them and invade their privacy. But, if you have something customers want, you are not "bugging" them—you are serving them!

When you decide to be an owner, there is always more you can do. Don't stop with one idea. Don't be a victim of that one idea not working for you. That's a typical response: "We tried that! It didn't work." Well, what else did you try?

To picture what it is to be an owner, picture one of those little windup toys that has a sensor knob in the front so that whenever it bumps into something it turns 30 degrees and starts off again. If you put that toy in a room with an open door, it will always find its way out of the room because every time it hits a wall it just turns and starts again. It might be called an "Owner Toy," because that's what being an owner is. A victim toy hits a wall and stalls and then runs out of battery. It sits in the room until someone either finds it or steps on it, breaking it forever.

So don't stop with one idea. One good idea is still only one idea. For poor Richard, the car wash card was a good start, but not a complete marketing plan. Now another nice guy is out of business.

"Now I have to find another place to wash my car," Sam concluded. "And I'm sure a couple hundred people will wish that Richard's detail shop was still around when July hits. A simple letter, postcard, or phone call could have saved that business and probably built it bigger for next year. It's sad."

Time Management Is Ownership

People really don't manage time so much as they own their energy. They make investments of energy based on taking ownership of their commitments and agreements and, especially, promises of achievement they have made to themselves. Here are four time management quotes we love, and we recommend that you copy at least two that you like and put them up in your workspace and watch what happens when they are metabolized and internalized into your subconscious mind!

> *"Start by doing*
> *what's necessary,*
> *then what's possible,*
> *and suddenly*
> *you are doing the impossible."*
> —St. Francis of Assisi

Start the day by doing what you know needs to be done. That's what's necessary. Do that. Then you will enter the realm of possibility.

What's possible? We want to double our income this month compared to last month. What are the possibilities? What are possible actions we could take to do that? And now that a few of those are in progress, it's time to think way out of the box. Maybe I could even get my key people together to do a two-hour session on *The Impossible*. What great windfall profit ideas do we think of as impossible? Let's list a series of impossible things, and then ask, "What if we *had* to do this?"

Many of the great breakthroughs in business innovation that owners have created are activities that victims thought were impossible.

***

> *"Learn to use ten minutes*
> *intelligently.*
> *It will pay you huge*
> *dividends."*
> —William A. Irwin

Owners like to think in terms of 10 minutes. What can I use this 10-minute period for that would really move things forward? Victims, on the other hand, see 10 minutes as a waste. It's only 10 minutes, might as well just shoot the breeze, gossip, talk sports, complain about some people, make some personal phone calls, or even leave a little early today to beat the traffic.

If you have 10 minutes, own those minutes. Many breakthroughs have occurred in 10 minutes. Many great agreements have been made. Many powerful decisions to move forward have been made in 10 minutes. Many a relationship has been healed in a 10-minute conversation.

* * *

> *"You will never 'find'*
> *time for anything,*
> *if you want time you*
> *must make it."*
> —Charles Buxton

When we coach small business people who are victims, the real fun begins when we can show them that there is a whole new way to think about everything. Everything! Even time itself. Because when a victim starts going off about not being able to "find the time" to do any of our ideas that would improve (or even save) the business, we must re-orient them. We tell them: "You own time, or it owns you. Your choice! And if you choose to own time, then you can do anything you want."

It's really not the truth that victims "can't find time" to do something. What they really can't find is the *will* to do it. Once they see that, the power of choice opens up to them. If we had advised our car detailer Richard to spend two hours a day sending and delivering invitations to his customers, he probably would have said that he wouldn't have time to do that. Given all the pressing hassles, he wouldn't be able to see how he could find the time. But what if we had upped the ante? What if we had told Richard that we'd give him a million dollars in tax-free cash if he spent two weeks doing it? Would he turn us down? Not likely. He'd more likely say, "Wow, I'll make time!"

How does this happen? How does a person make time for something? If your employee falls off a stool and hits her head on the floor and is bleeding, can you find the time to attend to her and call an ambulance? Or do you later tell her grieving parents that you couldn't find the time?

One of the truths a small business owner, a true *owner*, wakes up to is that there *is* time enough to succeed. If you view the time in your day with rigorous self-honesty, then time is no longer a problem. Priorities are your problem, not time.

The owner is different from the victim in this vital relationship to priorities. The owner prioritizes the success of the business. It comes first, ahead of all other activities during the workday.

The victim, on the other hand, prioritizes nothing. The victim just gets pushed and pulled all day by circumstance and other people's complaints and needs. Any head popping into the victim's office saying, "Gotta minute?" is the victim's newest and highest priority—any call coming in and beep from the computer alerting him to an e-mail waiting, anything, anyone. That's his newest high priority.

Meanwhile, the owner is off-site planning his or her next quarter. The owner is in seclusion, with no interruptions, working *on* the business. When the owner wants to experience the business firsthand, it is at a time of the owner's choosing, not some panicky response to being "shorthanded" today. The owner owns priority.

* * *

> *"You have more to do
> than you can possibly do.
> You just need to feel good
> about your choices."*
> —David Allen

Victims are victims of their own to-do lists. They make the list up, stare at the multitude of tasks to be done, and feel overwhelmed. They think to themselves, "I have more to do than I can possibly get done." That thought alone acts as a central nervous system depressant. Just thinking "I have more to do than I can possibly get done" causes the victim to lose energy. Soon a huge sense of fatigue sets in. Consciousness clouds over. Weariness and depression set in. The victim looks back down at the list and picks it up in a limp hand and then tosses it down. When someone peeks in at the victim and asks, "Do you have a minute?" the victim says, "Of course." Now the victim talks for 20 minutes about something not even on the list! It gets worse, and there's no end to this.

The owner realizes something that this victim does not realize. Time management is not a matter of managing tasks, or time, or learning to multitask, or becoming more organized, or any of that. Time management is about courage. Plain and simple. It is a boldness issue, and only boldness will solve the problem of time management. Only courage will demolish that list.

God grant me the courage: (1) to delegate, (2) to reduce my list to three things for today, (3) to hold others accountable, (4) to hire capable people who would be flattered if I trusted them to do all these things on my list, (5) to hold myself accountable, (6) to be ruthless, (7) to be powerful and brave and (8) to be an *owner* and not a *victim*.

Owners Work *on* Their Businesses

Here's another way to understand the owner/victim dichotomy: Owners work *on* their businesses and victims work *in* their businesses.

This is a powerful insight first introduced by Michael Gerber in his "E Myth" series of books (for great books such as this to help you boost your business, see our Recommended Readings section in the back of this book or visit our Website at *www.smallbusinesstruth.com*). Michael Gerber revolutionized the way small business owners approach their jobs, and we recommend his books highly. Sam has brought Gerber in to speak to various client groups, always with great, transformative results.

Gerber's work dramatizes the fact that the biggest mistake made by people who start their own small businesses is that they end up working IN that business instead of working ON the business. These people have become victims of their own creation. (Ever hear of the madman in the insane asylum who is given crayons in the morning to express himself with who draws a horrific monster on his pad, then looks at the monster, screams, jumps up from the table and runs out of the room. Is your business like this?)

To an owner, a business can be likened to a racehorse. An owner buys the racehorse, trains and cares for the racehorse, and then derives great pleasure from seeing the racehorse race and win.

To a victim, it's different. The victim has also bought a horse, but the victim straps himself to the underside of the horse (his business) and then is taken for a terrifying ride.

The owner uses his business to obtain wealth. The victim is used *by* his business, in fact used *up* by his business, leaving it at the end of the day worn out and wondering, "What was I thinking getting into this business? It's such a drain."

The owner takes full responsibility for his business's success. Full responsibility! The victim blames circumstance for the business's struggles.

The owner lives from the inside out, going deep inside to connect with his or her goals and dreams each day. The victim lives from the outside in, going to work and fighting off fires and solving outside problems pressing in on him or her, *as if he or she is employed by the business* instead of the other way around.

Owners take ownership of their energy and creativity as they are applied to their business. Owners *own* their businesses! Owners own their numbers; victims often don't even want to see them.

You can stop being a victim and take ownership at any moment. It is a miracle when it happens (a miracle we observe every day), but it is not all that difficult. It does not require new traits and characteristics on the part of the owner, because it is a choice. The owner/victim distinction lives at the level of choice. Make the choice and you can choose ownership. Refuse to choose and you'll be a victim by default.

Victims no longer can see that their businesses are a creation of theirs! They can no longer experience the business as a personally crafted, ongoing work in progress. Instead they see it as a fixed entity that they have to go be a slave to. The creator has become a creature!

Victims feel beat-up. They feel beat-up by their customers and frightened by their competition. They feel betrayed by their employees. Victims soon feel misunderstood and under-appreciated by their spouses. ("If she only realized what I go through every day to keep this thing afloat!")

Victims live a life based on fear. ("What do I dread today?")

Owners live a life based on love. ("What would I love to make happen?")

A victim wakes up and asks him or herself, "What do I hope doesn't happen today?"

An owner starts the day consulting his or her goal sheet. ("What would I love to produce today?")

Anyone can live as a victim, and anyone can live as an owner. It's just a matter of the questions you ask. We all live inside one inquiry or another. Is your inquiry there by choice? Or has it chosen you? What questions do you want to be asking yourself? Those questions will determine whether you are working in your business or on it. The inquiry you live inside is what determines your behavior.

An owner asks these questions:

$ "How can I use this circumstance to my advantage?"

$ "How can I differentiate myself in the customer's eyes?"

$ "What's something creative and exciting I can do this week to get my people and my customers talking?"

$ "What value can I add that would allow a price increase and that the customer would really appreciate?"

$ "What steps can I take to really grow this thing?"

$ "What outcome would I like to produce this month?"

$ "What would be a creative and exciting way to get that result?"

$ "How can I help my people? How can I help my customer more?"

A victim asks questions such as:

$ "When will I ever get caught up so I can get out of here?"

$ "How much will this new competitor hurt me?"

$ "Why do I feel that I have to be a babysitter to my own people?"

$ "Why can't you get good employees these days?"

$ "How long does it take for a business to start turning a profit?"

$ "Why is it that the harder I work, the deeper in debt we go?"

$ "Why can't I trust these customers?"

$ "Why is it that all these expensive ads I run do nothing for me?"

$ "When do I start liking this work?"

$ "What was I thinking when I started this business?"

$ "Why doesn't anyone ever tell you how hard it is?"

$ "Why didn't I wait until I had more capital to start this business with?"

Don't Violate Your Own Dream

When you started your business you were living a dream. If you remember to remain an owner, you will honor that dream every day. You will see your business growth as a form of lucid dreaming. Each day you will use your imagination to craft more progress.

Owners dream all day long and turn each dream into an action plan.

Victims only dream at night.

"Those who dream at night in the dusty recesses of their minds wake in the day to find that all was vanity," said T.E. Lawrence (Lawrence of Arabia). "But the dreamers of the day are dangerous people, for they may act their dream with open eyes, and make it possible."

Even victims can remember way back when they had their daytime dream going on. They set up their business, they remember, to get certain things out of it. But when the first wave of fear hit, and they became victims, the dream vanished and the nightmare began. It turned into more work than they thought and less money than they hoped for. It had them accepting the myth that "you'll never turn a profit until you've been in it for four years."

Once the victim position is taken, all of these nine lies become easy to believe and repeat. They are what *explains* the victim position. They are the rationale.

Victims put all the good things they used to imagine into the vague and unreal future, or the distant past.

Owners seize the moment.

Victims think of a lot of things they "should" be doing to improve their business, but they are just too busy to do them now. (They'll do that price increase in the future. They'll recruit that great new person when they are less busy. They'll work up that fun special event to show appreciation to customers when they can get some room to think. They'll fix up the location and paint some areas when they get a break from the *grind of survival*.)

Victims are focused on survival, whereas owners are focused on the next quantum leaps of success. (In small business life, what you focus on grows.)

The owner does all these good things now. Now is when it all happens. And if it can't literally happen now, an owner sets precise deadlines. Sets the deadlines now. He and she set the deadlines now, so that they are still in the now. Deadlines soon become the owner's best friend: "We're changing our price structure January 1. We are hiring our new marketing director by March 15. We are going to have the building painted and made over by April 30. We will have the whole neighborhood papered with our new flier by noon on Friday."

Victims are victims of their own cynicism. They bring a negative, fatalistic "what can you possibly do?" approach to work every day, and it becomes fatal to their business.

Own Your Creative Responses

Victim bosses spend their time inside their businesses reacting to everything and everyone. They do not understand that it's powerful to empower others to run things. One of the myths we have to dispel is that empowering others means you're not in charge. The truth is, the more time you're spending floating around, looking over people's shoulders, the more you cause your people to think, "We're in crisis, even the owner's here all the time trying to keep this thing afloat!"

Unfortunately, many business managers are secretly happy when they say, "This place would fall apart without me." They get their whole identity from being a business owner, from being the boss. So they really want that sense of importance, that sense of "I am needed at this business." And secretly, they don't want to leave the business, because they're trying to get their self-esteem from the wrong source, from thinking, "I'm so important that, even if the business isn't doing great financially, I'm still the boss of something, so this is my place."

These business managers are like the parents whose kids are about to leave home for good and say, "What do I do, now? I have no identity!" Or the person who's worked his whole life for one company and retires, and after that feels useless, and has nothing to live for, and starts carrying the empty briefcase back into the workplace and company security has to escort him out!

A lot of business owners have descended into that dysfunctional belief that "It's all me, it's all me." They fail to grasp that their business is really just a tool that exists to serve them—not the other way around.

People that self-centered on their business are going to miss opportunities to duplicate themselves. The first thing they say when you bring duplication up as a concept is, "My business isn't big enough to have a second person, and I can't possibly devote more hours of the day—that won't work." But there may be duplication opportunities to sell within your business that don't actually require someone actually doing the work.

The following is an interesting an example of opportunity seized. Diane was a personal exercise trainer we know. Obviously, she is in a very one-on-one business. But there was an innovative way she's figured out to duplicate herself.

As do most personal trainers, Diane would show up in someone's work out area, such as their house or a gym, and go through the routines with them. But what she figured out was that most of the clients she was getting didn't necessarily need her to be physically there to tell them how to work out, because they pretty much knew how to work out. After they got their routines down, they were using her as a source of motivation, because if someone was watching, they were more accountable. If someone was watching, they would actually work out!

So Diane decided to duplicate herself. She started with planning.

"Here are the different plans I have," she would tell prospective customers. "First, I have a plan where I will come here three times per week and work out with you, at a fixed fee per month. And I also have another plan—in this case I could come on one of these three days of the week—it could be Monday, Wednesday, or Friday—to meet you at the gym to work out, but you won't know which day it will be. I will only come once weekly, so you're going to go to the gym, ready to work out, and wait for me to go work out with you. But if I don't show up, guess what? You're already down at the gym, dressed and waiting, so you're going to start working out anyway. You're not going to say, 'Well, Diane's not here. I'm going home.'"

The second plan worked because the real inertia she found with most of her clients was getting them to go down to the gym. In this way she was able to duplicate herself, even though it wasn't the typical way that people would think of duplication. There are different ways you can duplicate your business. And technology gives you a great advantage to duplicate yourself. And if you look at the things your business does, there are areas of the business that can be duplicated. Consider opening a second or third location. That's a way to take the actual business and duplicate another copy of it somewhere else.

And if you look at areas inside the business, you can also find things that are possible to duplicate using technology that can be very profitable. There are possibilities for you to duplicate customer service, maintenance, automatic e-mail services, and dial-in services—there are packages that really lend themselves well to all types of duplication. The key is to really look in the business and ask, "Does this have the potential of duplication?"

Victims live in tyranny.

It is the tyranny of the urgent.

Victims Are Always Addressing Themselves to Urgent Matters

"Whaaat? Who's on the phone? Tell him to hold I'm trying to work with this customer!—Hey, hey, tell that vendor to NOT PULL HIS TRUCK UP FRONT LIKE THAT!!!!—Wait Willie, where are you going? NO! I said you could have *this afternoon* off not this morning—Where is my Blackberry? Anybody see it? I'm late to a meeting with the attorney—Mary! Mary! Call the attorney for me—What? Just a MINUTE!"

The tyranny of the urgent is the primary force in the victim's life. His energy and attention are devoted to urgent matters throughout the day, and he does whatever looks most urgent at the moment.

But in a small business, life is separated between two categories: The Urgent and The Important. The owner works on what's important: "It may be urgent to take this phone call, but it's more *important* to design this new marketing strategy, so the phone call will wait until I do all my phoning at 11 a.m." The owner is in control. The owner works on the important things and leaves the urgent things to others.

The victim is always thinking about the important things, but they are nagging background thoughts as he or she addresses the urgent throughout the day.

The owner helps him or herself live in the land of the important by writing goals down and having those goals dictate his choice of action. The owner is wary of the urgent and knows that the urgent can undermine every goal he has.

By surrendering to the urgent, the victim feels very busy. What's this phone call? What's this customer want? What is my employee complaining about? It feels so very busy! "I feel like I've put in quite a day!" What a day, what a day.

Later that night the victim confesses to a spouse, "But what I did today was not very important. I did a lot of urgent things, but nothing important, nothing that's going to move us forward."

The victim thinks the owner has the advantage of discipline. If a victim observes an owner in action, he makes a mental note that "that person is more *disciplined* than I am, it's a trait, a characteristic, that I don't have. Wish I did." But the owner knows different. The owner knows that discipline is merely *remembering what you want.*

Conclusion

You Can
Handle the Truth

If you start me up,
If you start me up I'll never stop
—The Rolling Stones

Why did you go into your business to begin with? What was the original dream? Independence? Freedom? Wealth? Lots of vacation time? An exciting adventure, and a sense of winning at life?

Go back to before you started and recreate that dream. List all the benefits you imagined there would be. List the benefits to yourself and to all the people close to you. Be precise about the benefits of your business succeeding in a big way. Don't hide that list or repress that dream, because it will be the source of your *want to*. It will get you up in the morning and lift your thinking all day. Dreams have a function. They are there to start you up!

Then, once you know the truth about how small businesses succeed, you will apply that truth to your own business and succeed in ways you never dreamed of. Your dream will start you up. But after the first year of following these principles you'll realize that you're just getting started!

Let your dream fuel the ride.

Soon you'll see how clear and easy it is. There are only two gears driving your business mindset: (1) knowing the truth and (2) applying the truth.

The best way to know, really *know,* the truth about anything is to first eliminate and discard what's not true. That's why we wrote this book in the format we did. We knew from our experience coaching people that it is far more effective to let a person show you what is *not* working before you show him or her what does work. It makes it far easier to understand something if you can clearly see how you've gone wrong and why.

Doing it wrong is the best teacher you have! Uncovering these lies and revealing them to be *lies* is the best way we have to dramatize the true way to success.

Sam talks about business being a game you enter. And if you play the game with a certain level of passion and attention, your whole life will change—not just from the reward of money for winning the game, but from something much bigger than that.

"A lot of people think business 'success' is just a business making a good profit, and that's it," Sam said. "I don't believe that. I think your success becomes a way of living."

The only real enemy you've got is your own fear. Notice the feeling in your gut as you go back and re-read these nine truths. Do you feel some butterflies? Good! That's the fear. Know it for what it is, because by boldly stepping forward with the truth you will eliminate all fear from your business.

Be True and They'll Come Back to You

"You don't want to build a business that you're afraid of," says Sam. "You don't want to always be afraid of something bad happening and losing everything. We all hear those stories, the person who makes it big and then loses it all, right? Those stories are where the fear comes from. You can't succeed with that fear in you. You have to know for certain that if you practice a certain way of living—a fearless search for the real truth—that you can get everything you ever wanted from your business! Once you shift from being a victim to being a true owner, then you have something that people can't take away from you. You are the person who created that! And you own the fact that it's created from what is inside you. Not from all the external things that just happened to work in a certain way. And there's a huge power in knowing that if, for some reason, something did happen, your customers will respect you and will come back to you."

Once you take this level of true ownership you realize that you *can* handle the truth: the truth of what you will see in one year of using these principles.

For example, you will look back and see more customers and more profit simply by having used the truth of the

Open Hand. One year from now you will see that raising prices and raising value at the same time increased your business! You will see that your business is just a reflection of who you are. If you are confident and generous, your business will be solid and profitable.

Follow these principles and you will see that you can get the customers you *want*, not the customers you think you need. These principles will shift that for you. Everything you do will be because it's something you *want* to do, not something you *need* to do. Your whole life will elevate to a life of wants, desires, and intention, away from the old life of needs, fears, and obligation. That's what the truth will do for you.

Recommended Reading

Blasingame, Jim. *Small Business Is Like a Bunch of Bananas*. Ala.: SBN Books, 2001.

Canfield, Jack, et al. *The Power of Focus.* Fla.: HCI, 2000.

Chandler, Steve, and Scott Richardson. *100 Ways to Motivate Others*. Franklin Lakes, New Jersey: Career Press, 2004.

Checketts, Darby. *Customer Astonishment Handbook.* Cornerstone Pro-Dev Pr, 1998.

Dauten, Dale. *The Max Strategy.* New York: William Morrow & Company, 1996.

Gerber, Michael E. *The E-Myth Revisited*. New York: HarperCollins, 1995.

Kennedy, Dan. *No B.S. Business Success.* Irvine, Calif.: Entrepreneur Press, 2004.

Maher, Barry. *Getting the Most From Your Yellow Pages Advertising.* Mass.: Aegis Publishing Group, 1997.

Ries, Al, and Jack Trout. *Positioning: The Battle for Your Mind*. New York: McGraw-Hill, 2000.

Rohn, Jim. *Seven Strategies for Wealth & Happiness.* New York: Prima Lifestyles, 1988.

Stanley, Thomas J., and William J. Danko. *The Millionaire Next Door.* New York: Simon & Schuster, 1996.

Index

About the Authors

Sam Beckford is the founder of eight small businesses. The first five were massive failures. After business number five he decided to get a "real job," but thankfully got fired after five months and started business number six, which made him a millionaire. Sam has shared his business strategies and philosophy with thousands of other small business owners and has personally helped hundreds of business owners across North America increase their personal income by an additional $40,000 per year while working less. Sam lives in Vancouver, Canada, with his wife Valerie and daughter Isabella. You can contact Sam Beckford at *www.smallbusinesstruth.com*.

Steve Chandler is the author of *Reinventing Yourself* and a number of other international bestsellers in the personal growth field. He has coached and trained more than 30 Fortune 500 companies and hundreds of small businesses. He is a visiting faculty member in the Soul-Centered Leadership program at the University of Santa Monica and lives in Arizona with his wife Kathy and their pet Grizzly Bear.

Come join the authors!

You can help expand the success of your business by visiting our Website at *www.smallbusinesstruth.com* and obtaining a free CD and free articles, including *Small Business Lies Number 10 and 11* (available only to readers of this book—visit the site and mention this code: 999)! We would like to give you a demonstration of how *we* use the Open Hand concept to give our readers more than they expected.

You can read up on all the latest research Sam Beckford and Steve Chandler have done on how to strengthen your cash flow and turn your business into a powerhouse of profit. You'll be given options and opportunities for live events and personal and group coaching. You can also communicate with the authors directly via the Website, show them your advertising, and ask questions about your particular challenges.